Write Away 1

A Course for Writing English

Donald R. H. Byrd
Hunter College (CUNY)
CUNY Graduate School

Gloria Gallingane
La Guardia Community College (CUNY)

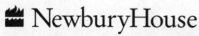 NewburyHouse
A Division of HarperCollins*Publishers*

Director: Laurie E. Likoff
Production Coordinator: Cynthia Funkhouser
Text and Cover Design: Ron Newcomer
Text Illustratons: Carol Ann Gaffney and Anna Veltfort
Production: R. David Newcomer Associates
Compositor: CFW Graphics
Printer and Binder: Malloy Lithographing, Inc.

NEWBURY HOUSE
A division of HarperCollins Publishers

Language Science
Language Teaching
Language Learning

Write Away 1: A Course for Writing English

Library of Congress Cataloging-in-Publication Data
(Revised for vol. 1)

Byrd, Donald R. H.
    Write away.

    1. English language—Textbooks for foreign speakers.
2. English language—Rhetoric.   I. Gallingane, Gloria.
II. Title.
PE1128.B85   1990   428.2'4   89-13290
ISBN 0-06-041087-6 (v. 1)
ISBN 0-06-041088-4 (v. 2)
ISBN 0-06-41089-2 (v. 3)

94 93 92 91   9 8 7 5 4 3 2 1

Acknowledgments

Working with other people sweetens the task of writing textbooks. *Write Away* is the result of a long collaboration that has been often tested. I am indebted to Gloria Gallingane for her abiding commitment to these materials, a commitment I shared. Seeing them so successfully used by teachers and students certainly helped to make our experience and theories about teaching writing real. The names of the people I particularly wish to thank include: Effie Cochran, Rena Deutsch, Joan Dye, Nancy Frankfort, Cindy Funkhouser, Jack Gantzer, Nancy Gross, Jann Huizenga, Judy Gex, Laurie Likoff, Grace Martinez, Robert Miller, Ron Newcomer, Ann Raimes, Ken Sheppard, Rick Shur, Carolyn Sterling, Howard Stitzer, and Stanley Zelinski. Two people especially enrich and give purpose to my life: Sarah Henderson Byrd Flanagan and Athanassios Doumanidis. To them I lovingly dedicate this book.

Donald R. H. Byrd

Co-authors of texts develop their own *modus operandi* and this holds true for the two authors of this three-book *Write Away* series. In planning for the revison and expansion of the original two-book series into three, Dr. Donald R. H. Byrd and I decided that he would assume responsibility for Book 3, I would revise Book 2, and together we would recreate Book 1; a division of labor well-suited to our busy professional lives. Dr. Byrd is and has been an excellent role model as a textbook writer, indefatigable and creative, and I want to thank him first and foremost for his enthusiasm and dedication to this project. Thanks also to members of our editorial staff at Newbury House, and to Ron Newcomer, our West Coast editor, for their infinite patience. And sincere thanks to the following friends and colleagues who, through comments and suggestions, have directly influenced some of the units in this series: Pamela Breyer, Irene Dutra, Winifred Falcon, Gary Gabriel, Jean McConochie, and Ellen Shaw. Finally, this book is dedicated to the memory of James E. Weaver, whose teaching and materials inspired countless young and inexperienced ESL teachers and always impressed his colleagues. His untimely death in 1984 is still mourned by his many friends and former students.

Gloria Gallingane

Photo Credits

Contents

Unit 7 **Early Morning Help**
COMBINING SENTENCES AND REWRITING

Unit 8 **The Concert**
REWRITING A MODEL PARAGRAPH

Unit 9 **Did You Know That . . . ?**
REWRITING A MODEL PARAGRAPH

Unit 10 **Miriam's Routine**
REWRITING A MODEL PARAGRAPH

Unit 30   **The Judo Teacher**   171
REWRITING A MODEL PARAGRAPH

Unit 31   **The House Husband**   177
COMBINING SENTENCES

Unit 32   **Let's Eat**   183
REWRITING A MODEL PARAGRAPH

Introduction

Write Away is a three-book series for students of English. The series helps students write English better through an integrative four-skill approach and through specially designed guided-to-free exercises.

The three books progress in grammatical, lexical, and rhetorical difficulty either by isolating specific points for writing practice or by allowing students to experiment with various means of expression through sentence combinations.

The *Write Away* approach views writing, like other language skills, as the acquisition and mastery of various components ("isolates") that fit together as a whole in communication.

Written English, after all, is communication, and writing is a skill that connects with other language skills. In *Write Away* this connection is deliberately exploited. In fact, this holistic treatment is an integral part of the *Write Away* approach as revealed in the sequence of exercises. Although the exercises always lead to a well-formed composition, they treat more than just writing skills *per se*.

The topics in *Write Away* were chosen according to these general criteria: (1) the intrinsic interest of the content; (2) accurate reflection of the real world; (3) appropriateness to the students' needs; (4) potential for getting students to react; and (5) suitability to serve as a basis for language expansion. These topics, at times, entertain, inform, or gently provoke—but never offend or insult. Classroom piloting of the materials helped to eliminate undesirable topics. The students, therefore, should be allowed and encouraged to react orally through discussions and brainstorming before they write.

The Organization of *Write Away* Units

Students and teachers will quickly become familiar with the "friendly" layout of *Write Away,* the pleasant illustrations and airy design, the developmental sequence of exercises that lead to the end product, and the clear focus of the exercises.

The first exercises in each *Write Away* unit focus on vocabulary expansion and reading comprehension. The purpose of these exercises is to introduce the "access" vocabulary and the ideas needed for the subsequent writing practice. Access vocabulary refers to those pivotal words that are needed for a clear understanding and discussion of the topic, whether in speech or in writing. It is not surprising, then, that these new words are defined very specifically in the exercises — only as they are used in the unit. We opted for this streamlined treatment of word meaning because further dictionary colorings would only bewilder students at this stage.

The second skill that *Write Away* treats is reading. The reading exercises are receptive; that is, they do not require the student to produce any new information. Using tasks such as matching, multiple choice, fill-in, and sequencing, students are tested as to how well they understand the content of the unit. These exercises (Exercise C) are called "Reading Check," and they are positioned just after the model paragraph or the sentences to be combined (Exercise B). Exercise D provides the focused writing activity.

Invariably students, through their own experience, will know something about the topic, and the initial exercises tap and expand that knowledge. The exercises are most effectively used by having the students, without the intrusion of the teacher, compare their answers to the exercises *before* and *after* they read. This comparison reveals, in a general way, students' progress in understanding the ideas and in recognizing the vocabulary in the unit.

Exercise D in each *Write Away* unit is the "core" writing activity — usually one of two task types: *rewriting* of a model composition (usually a paragraph); or *combining* short sentences that are parts of longer, natural-sounding stretches of discourse. As the writing exercises are laid out developmentally in a single unit, students are expected to use a mixture of rewriting and combining operations. These operations might be likened to various "revising" efforts, with the developed composition being the final result. *Write Away* anticipates what the end composition should look like and, through a choice of focused exercises, guides students through the processes that produce a well-formed composition.

Throughout the vocabulary, reading, and writing exercises, students are led through a sequence of tasks, from recognition to production. The first tasks of each unit are for recognition purposes only. They do two things: present access vocabulary intrinsic to the unit; and check the reading comprehension of the ideas contained in the unit. After students become familiar with the vocabulary and the content, they are ready to start the production tasks of writing.

Following all focused writing practice (through paragraph rewriting or sentence combining), there is a culminating free, individualized composition assignment (Exercise E "Writing Follow-Up"). This composition is the moment of truth, for the entire value of the previously executed exercises in the unit are put to the test. The essential purpose of the previous practice was to prepare the students for this ultimate stage of composing. Predictably, the topics suggested for "Writing Follow-Up" are thematically, rhetorically, and grammatically related to the previous parts of the unit. Students, after the concentrated analysis and revision of the model composition, easily make the transition to composing on their own, going from analysis and manipulation to analogy. To ensure this transition, there are guided questions to encourage the students to put their own ideas on paper —either in class overseen by the teacher or as homework.

The Role of the Teacher in Using *Write Away*

Some roles a teacher or tutor may assume while using *Write Away* include these: *facilitator/expeditor* (making sure circumstances, reference materials, and classroom set-up are conducive to writing); *monitor* (being available to answer questions when solicited); *pacer* (keeping the students on task within time constraints); *nurturer* (making the students feel good about their own writing accomplishments); and *participant* (showing a personal interest in the students' ideas and ways of expression).

The design of the materials in *Write Away,* since they foster student autonomy, are easily used in all individualized learning situations, such as learning and literacy centers and, especially, in writing laboratories. Whether in the hands of an experienced or inexperienced teacher, a trained or untrained tutor, the exercises are easily used and are non-threatening. However, it is most important that the teacher or tutor not let the writing practice become tedious or tiresome. Vigilance is necessary to ensure that the focused writing practice does not become an end in itself. An almost certain invitation to ennui is to treat the practice as methodical or routine. The writing exercises are seen as means to an end — not an end unto themselves. Their purpose is for students to end up with an acceptable, well-formed, cohesive composition.

Naturally the teacher, being the expert, must judge which practice activities the students need. The teacher should also decide on the kinds of activities for different students (since individual needs vary), how these activities are to be done (in pairs, in groups, with individuals, or as a whole class), and how much time to allow for the various sequences (most units should take no more than an hour or two, at most, excluding the homework assignment that follows).

Generally students like to talk about the ideas they encounter, and the judicious teacher will not only allow students to talk but will build in discussion activities in each class. This free — and certainly spontaneous — exchange of ideas allows students to practice their oral expression without the intrusion of grammatical and vocabulary rules. These times of expression also serve to humanize the writing class.

The *Write Away* System

The exercises in *Write Away* are grammatically focused and are always meaningfully contextualized. Students will be able to use their understanding of the content to sharpen their grammatical accuracy. The system developed for *Write Away* resulted from a unique analysis of the various grammatical operations that a writer utilizes when writing and revising. As stated earlier, the advantage of using *Write Away* is that these grammatical operations in writing and revising are anticipated and laid out in the sequence of each unit. The results of the operations applied in sequence will produce a well-formed composition.

There are a variety of ways to express oneself. *Write Away* has codified these ways, called operations, into four categories: (1) inflectional; (2) coordinative; (3) subordinative; and (4) derivational. Any well-formed composition contains a mixture of these grammatical operations. If any operation is faulty, it is distracting, sidetracking the reader from the *what* of expression to the *how*. These operations, then, are not seen as ends unto themselves. Rather, they should be seen as the means to the end of clear expression. They provide the *how* of expression so that the *what* of expression is clear.

(1)   *Inflectional* writing operations are the most fundamental parts of English grammar. Inflectional endings are important elements

in standard English. The parts of speech in English that inflect are: nouns, verbs, adjectives and adverbs, and pronouns.

(2) *Coordinative* operations use such words as *and, but,* and *or,* and they serve to join equal elements together like single words (*boys and girls, he and she, blue and yellow*), phrases (*She dances and swims well, . . . out of sight and out of mind*), and clauses (*He danced with Mary, but he didn't dance with Helen*).

Coordinative operations are good ways to put short sentences and sentence parts together to form longer, more complex structural hierarchies. This way writers avoid short, unnatural staccato sentences that tire the reader. Coordinative operations, then, help to make one's writing smooth and flowing, and they, along with subordinative operations, frequently occur in the numerous sentence combining exercises in *Write Away*.

(3) *Subordinative* operations include the insertion of words or clauses that modify, describe, or amplify in some way different sentence parts: adjective words, phrases, or clauses that modify nouns; and adverb words, phrases, or clauses that modify verbs, adjectives, or other adverbs. Noun clauses are discussed below.

The simplest subordinative maneuver is the insertion of a single-word adjective or adverb as in these examples: *blue book; he ran quickly.* There are, of course, more complex subordinative operatons, like the insertion of adjective phrases as in *that book on the desk* or the adverb phrases as in *He ran like a rabbit.*

The most complicated subordinative procedure occurs with clauses because of various reference, syntactic, or other concomitant grammatical considerations. Basically, there are two kinds of clausal subordination: adjective (relative) clauses (usually with *who(m), that,* or *which*) and adverb clauses (using such subordinating conjunctions as *because, although, even though, since, while, when, as soon as, until,* and so on).

Noun clauses with *wh-* words (*What he said was regrettable*) or *that* (*It is regrettable that he said that*)—although they are not technically subordinative structures—are treated in *Write Away* as subordinative operations since they, like the subordinative structures above, are the product of the union of two elements, one of which is relegated to a dependent syntactic status. Noun clauses, like adjective and adverb clauses, share the characteristic of being dependent clauses. In the case of noun clauses, however, they form a higher level constituent that, like dependent clauses, needs the rest of the sentence. In other words, noun clauses, like adjective and adverb clauses, cannot stand alone isolated from the rest of the sentence.

(4) *Derivational* operations occur when one part of speech changes, usually through suffixation, to another part of speech. Such lexical derivations include changes from a verb to a noun (*teach/teacher, assist/assistant*), an adjective to a noun (*happy/happiness, true/truth, different/difference*), an adjective to an adverb (*extreme/extremely*), a noun to a verb (*analysis/analyze, mystery, mystify*), and from a noun to an adjective (*child/childish, hope/hopeful*). There are some derivational prefixes that occur in English as in *danger/endanger,* where the noun is changed to a verb.

A good dictionary is a valuable tool for students when they are unsure of the derivational contrasts of words. It is not sufficient, however, merely to be aware of the different derivations of words in isolation; one also has to know how the derived forms are used in sentences. Learners need to know specifically which function words cluster with the different derivations. A complete learner's dictionary will show not only the different derivations of words but will also show through examples how these variations are used in stretches of language. For example, when using the different derivations of *interest,* the student also has to know that *in* follows the adjective *interested* as in the sentence, "I am *interested in* art," or that *to* follows the adjective *interesting* as in the sentence "Art is *interesting to* me."

To the Student

Every language has its own grammatical system. *Write Away* deals with the grammatical system of written English. In order to help students write better, *Write Away* uses a special approach based on our analysis of written English.

Certain operations are in all written English sentences. In writing, as in speaking and other language skills, there is a variety of ways to say the same idea. In most cases, a fluent speaker may use any one or more of these ways to express the same idea.

The following four sentences represent the operations:

1. They drive taxis on the weekends.
2. They are taxi drivers on the weekend
3. He drives a taxi on the weekends, and she does, too.
4. She and he drive taxis on the weekends.

If you analyze the meaning of each sentence above, you will see that all four contain approximately the same information as below:

Who does this?	two people
What do they do?	drive taxis
When do they do it?	on the weekends

In each sentence the same information is presented in a different manner, using different grammatical ways. In *Write Away*, there will be many opportunities to write sentences like these examples.

In *Write Away* there are vocabulary and reading exercises before the writing exercises. These exercises help you to become familiar with the new words and ideas in the unit. You will probably want to talk about the ideas with your classmates.

After you become familiar with the new words and ideas in each unit, it is time to practice writing. There are two kinds of writing exercises: rewriting a model composition, and sentence combining.

A Rewriting Example

Rewriting exercises involves writing a model paragraph according to a sequence of instructions. When you finish the last rewriting exercise, you will end up with a well-formed composition. Here is an example of a rewriting exercise.

Princess of Rock

(1) Princess is a famous rock singer.   (2) She gives concerts all over the world.   (3) Many young people want to be like her. (4) She makes a lot of money.   (5) She owns a silver jet.   (6) She flies it herself.   (7) She lives like royalty.   (8) She remembers her poor childhood in Chicago.

Here are some typical *Write Away* exercises for the above model paragraph.

1.   Johnny Punk is a rock singer, too, but he is not like Princess. Write about him.

Your first sentence: **Johnny Punk isn't a famous rock singer.**

2.   Princess does not give concerts any more. She lives a quiet life in the country with her family. Write about her in the past.

Your first sentence: **Princess was a famous rock singer.**

3.   Princess's daughter Ruthie wants to be a rock singer like her mother when she grows up. Write about her in the future.

Your first sentence: **Ruthie is going to be a famous rock singer.**

4.   Rewrite the paragraph by combining the following sentences. Omit the numbers.

Combine (1) and (2) with **, who**.
Combine (3) and (4) with **because**.
Combine (5) and (6) with **, which**.

NOTE: Omit **it** *in (6).*

Combine (7) and (8) with **, but**.
In (8), change **her poor** to **the poverty of her**.

Exercise 1 practices certain grammatical points: the negative forms in the present tense, and the changes in nouns and pronouns from feminine to masculine. Exercise 2 focuses on the past tense endings. Exercise 3 treats the *going to* future with the auxiliary changes. These exercises give you grammatical practice of different points in meaningful situations. The whole writing activity comes together in Exercise 4. This final rewriting results in a natural composition. You can see the use of various words (like *but, who, because, which*), and word changes (like *poor/poverty*) that make the paragraph smoother and easier to read. The paragraph on the next page is the result.

Princess of Rock

Princess is a famous rock singer, who gives concerts all over the world. Many young people want to be like her because she makes a lot of money. She owns a silver jet, which she flies herself. She lives like royalty, but she remembers the poverty of her childhood in Chicago.

A Sentence-Combining Example

The second kind of activity in *Write Away* allows you to express yourself in your own way. Sentence-combining activities require you to put smaller sentences together to form more complex sentences that are easier to read. Here is an example of a sentence-combining activity.

The Liberation of Mrs. Denis

1. a. Mr. Denis is a clerk.
   b. He works in a post office.

2. a. He always eats dinner.
   b. He always eats it as soon as he gets home.

3. a. One day he came home.
   b. He was tired.
   c. He was hungry.
   d. His dinner was not ready.

4. a. Mrs. Denis was reading a book.
   b. The book was about women.
   c. It was about their liberation.

5. a. Mr. Denis got angry.
   b. He said that he was going to a restaurant.
   c. He was going there to eat.

6. a. Mrs. Denis asked him to be patient for a few minutes.
   b. She left the room.

7. a. He thought that she went to prepare dinner.
   b. After a few minutes she appeared.
   c. She was wearing her hat.
   d. She was wearing her coat.
   e. She was wearing her gloves.

8. a. She smiled.
   b. Her smile was sweet.
   c. She said, "I'm ready, dear. Where are we going to eat?"

In a sentence-combining activity, like the one above, you can combine the sentences in more than one way. For example, you can combine 1a and 1b in a number of ways, such as:

1. Mr. Denis is a postal clerk.
2. Mr. Denis is a clerk in the post office.
3. Mr. Denis is a clerk, who works in a post office.
4. Mr. Denis, a clerk, works in the post office.

The finished sentence-combining activity would look something like the following:

The Liberation of Mrs. Denis

Mr. Denis is a post office clerk. He always eats dinner as soon as he gets home. One day he came home, tired and hungry, but dinner was not ready. Mrs. Denis was reading a book about women's liberation. Mr. Denis got angry and said he was going to a restaurant to eat. Mrs. Denis asked him to be patient for a few minutes and left the room. He thought that she went to prepare dinner, but after a few minutes she appeared, wearing her hat, coat, and gloves. She smiled sweetly and said, "I'm ready, dear. Where are we going to eat?"

After you finish a sentence-combining activity, always check your work to see if the way you combined the sentences is natural sounding. You can check your work with the Answer Key, which the teacher has, or the teacher may check your work with you. In either case, the Answer Key shows the most natural combinations as written by native speakers. Not every possibility is in the Answer Key, however. If your combinations are different, check with your teacher.

We hope the exercises in *Write Away* help you improve your written English along with your other English skills. We also hope you have a pleasurable experience using *Write Away*. Now get out your paper and pen, and . . . *Write Away*.

Unit 1

My Nickname Is C.C.

A. Vocabulary Preview

Match the following:

f   1. nickname

_____   2. first name

_____   3. middle name

_____   4. current

_____   5. hobby

_____   6. address

a. given name

b. between first and last name

c. the location of your home

d. something to do for relaxation

e. now

f. friendly name

Use these verbs and nouns to complete the sentences that follow.

VERB:	design	dance	study	teach
NOUN:	designer	dancer	student	teacher

1. Rudolph Nureyev is a famous *dancer* .

    He likes to _____ in ballets.

2. Christian Dior, a famous _____, likes to

    _____ clothing.

3. In your English class, you are a _____; you

    are in the class to _____ English.

4. In your English class, your _____ is there

    to _____ you English.

B.   Read the following:

My Nickname Is C.C.

(1) My first name is Cecilia.   (2) My middle name is Ann.   (3) My last name is Edwards.   (4) My nickname is C.C.   (5) I am from Georgia.   (6) Now I live in Brooklyn, New York.   (7) My address is 18 Clermont Street.   (8) I am a student.   (9) I study art at Pratt Institute.   (10) I want to be a designer. (11) I want to design furniture. (12) My hobby is dancing. (13) I am a very good dancer.

Cecelia

FIRST NAME: Cecilia
MIDDLE NAME: Ann
LAST NAME: Edwards
NICKNAME: C.C.
PLACE OF ORIGIN: Georgia
PRESENT ADDRESS: Brooklyn, New York, at 18
     Clermont Street
JOB: student of art at Pratt Institute
FUTURE PLANS: to be a designer of furniture
HOBBY: dancing

C. Reading Check

Match the questions with the correct answers.

_____ 1. What is your first name?

_____ 2. What is your middle name?

_____ 3. What is your last name?

_____ 4. What is your nickname?

_____ 5. Where are you from?

_____ 6. What is your present address?

_____ 7. Where are you a student?

_____ 8. What is your hobby?

_____ 9. What are your future plans?

a. to be a designer
b. Cecilia
c. Georgia
d. Ann
e. 18 Clermont Street, Brooklyn, New York
f. at Pratt Institute
g. C.C.
h. Edwards
i. dancing

D. Write Away

1. Rewrite the paragraph in Part B. Use the information about Ricky. Use the contraction **I'm** in (5), (8), and (13).

Your first sentence: **My first name is Ricardo**

Ricky

FIRST NAME: Ricardo
MIDDLE NAME: Oscar
LAST NAME: Correale
NICKNAME: Ricky
PLACE OF ORIGIN: Argentina
PRESENT ADDRESS: San Diego, California,
    at 34 Montessa Lane
JOB: student of English at the University of California
FUTURE PLANS: to be a teacher of English
HOBBY: playing tennis

---

2. Write about C.C. Use the contraction **She's** in (5), (8), and (13).

Your first sentence: **Her first name is Cecilia.**

3. Write about Ricky. Use the contraction **He's** in (5), (8), and (13).

Your first sentence: **His first name is Ricardo.**

4. Rewrite the paragraph in Part B. Use the information about Peggy and Jay. Use the contraction **He's** in (5), (8), and (13).

Peggy

FIRST NAME: Bei
MIDDLE NAME: Ki
LAST NAME: Cao
NICKNAME: Peggy
PLACE OF ORIGIN: China
PRESENT ADDRESS: Montreal, Canada, at
    10 St. Catherine Street
JOB: student of English at McGill University
FUTURE PLANS: to be a teacher of English
HOBBY: playing the piano

Jay

FIRST NAME: Jei
MIDDLE NAME: Wei
LAST NAME: Cao
NICKNAME: Jay
PLACE OF ORIGIN: China
PRESENT ADDRESS: Montreal, Canada, at
    10 St. Catherine Street
JOB: student of English at McGill University
FUTURE PLANS: to be a teacher of English
HOBBY: playing the piano

Your first sentence: **Our first names are Bei and Jei.**

5. Write about Peggy and Jay. Use the contraction **They're** in (5), (8), and (13).

Your first sentence: **Their first names are Bei and Jei.**

6.   Rewrite the paragraph in Part B. Make the following changes. Do NOT write the numbers.

Combine (1), (2), and (3).

Your first sentence: **My name is Cecilia Ann Edwards**.

Do NOT change (4).
Combine (5), (6), and (7).
   Use the contraction **I'm** in (5).
   Between (5) and (6) use **, but**.
   Use **at** before (7). Do NOT write **My address is** in (7).
Combine (8) and (9).
   Use the contraction **I'm** in (8).
   Write **art** before **student** in (8). Do NOT write **I
      study art** in (9).
Write **furniture** before **designer** in (10). Do NOT
   write (11).
Combine (12) and (13) with **, and I think**.
   Use the contraction **I'm** in (13).

E.   Writing Follow-Up

Write a paragraph of introduction about yourself. Use the paragraph in Exercise 6 above as a model. Use your name as the title. Answer these questions in your paragraph:

What is your name?
What is your nickname?
Where are you from?
What is your present address?
What is your job?
What are your future plans?
What is your hobby?

_____

_____

_____

_____

_____

_____

_____

_____

_____

Unit 2
My Best Friend

A.   Vocabulary Preview

Cross out (X) the incorrect word.

1.   She has (blond   dark   b~~lue~~   auburn) hair.

2.   She has (blue   long   brown   green) eyes.

3.   She has a (loud   quiet   tall   nice) personality.

4.   She's (tall   short   medium height   quiet).

5.   Her hair is (long   short   curly   blond   quiet).

6.   She's a (good   nice   rather) (person   listener   friend   name).

B.   Read the following:

My Best Friend

(1) My friend's name is Mary Vida.   (2) I call her Vee.   (3) She's about 20 years old.   (4) She has blond hair.   (5) Her hair is long.   (6) She has blue eyes.   (7) She's about five feet, six inches tall.   (8) She has a nice personality.   (9) She isn't a loud person.   (10) She's quiet.   (11) She has a good sense of humor.   (12) She's a good listener.   (13) She's always there when I have a problem.   (14) That's what a friend is for.

C.   Reading Check

Match the questions with the correct answers.

——— 1. Who is Mary
         Vida?

——— 2. What is her
         nickname?

——— 3. How old is she?

——— 4. What color is
         her hair?

——— 5. What color are
         her eyes?

——— 6. How tall is she?

——— 7. What kind of
         person is she?

——— 8. Why do I like
         her?

a. quiet
b. She is a good
   listener.
c. blond
d. Vee
e. over five feet
f. blue
g. my friend
h. about 20

D.   Write Away

1.   Write about Mary's friend, Ellen. Mary calls her
"Ellie." She is in the photograph (on page 9) with Mary.
Her personality is like Mary's.

Your first sentence: **My friend's name is Ellen.**

2. Write about another friend: Arthur. Use the information below:

Your first sentence: **My friend's name is Arthur.**

LAST NAME: Lane
FIRST NAME: Arthur
NICKNAME: Art
AGE: 30
COLOR OF HAIR: Black
COLOR OF EYES: Brown
HEIGHT: 6′ 2″
COMMENTS: pleasant personality, not quiet, out-
    going, wonderful sense of humor, not a good lis-
    tener but always there for a friend.

---

3.   Rewrite the paragraph about Art's wife. Her name is Diana, but he calls her Di. She is like Princess Diana of England.

Your first sentence: **Art's wife's name is Diana.**

4.   Rewrite the paragraph in Part B. Make the following changes:

Combine (1) and (2) with **, but.**
Do NOT change (3).
Combine (4), (5), and (6).
    Write **long,** before **blond** in (4).
    Do NOT write **Her hair is** in (5).
    Write **and** before **blue eyes** in (6); do NOT write **She
        has** in (6).
Do NOT change (7).
Combine (8) and (9) with **, but.**
Write **In fact,** before (10); write **rather** before **quiet** in (10).

Combine (10) and (11) with **and**; do NOT write **She**
   in (11).
Combine (12) and (13) with **, and**.
Do NOT change (14).

E.   Writing Follow-Up

Write about your best friend. Use the paragraph in Exercise 4 above as a model. Use his/her name as the title. Answer these questions in your paragraph:

Who is your best friend?
What is his/her nickname?
How old is he/she?
What color is his/her hair?
What color are his/her eyes?
How tall is he/she?
What kind of person is he/she?
Why do you like him/her?

_____

_____

_____

_____

_____

_____

_____

_____

Unit 3
Bilingual

A.   Vocabulary Preview

Match the following:

<u>*C*</u>   1. bilingual

_____   2. Indic

_____   3. originally

_____   5. gypsies

_____   6. Romany

_____   7. lucky

a. traveling people originally from Iran and India

b. the language of the gypsies

c. knowing two languages

d. family of languages from India

e. fortunate, happy, by chance

f. first

B.   Read the following:

Bilingual

1. a. Annie is bilingual.
    b. Rose is bilingual.

NOTE: Use **and**.

2. a. That is, Annie speaks two languages well.
    b. That is, Rose speaks two languages well.

NOTE: Use **They**.

3. a. They speak English.
    b. They speak Romany.

NOTE: Use **and**.

4. a. Romany is an Indic language.
    b. It is originally from India.
    c. Most gypsies speak it.

NOTE: Do NOT write **It is** in b.
          Write **originally from India** after a.
          Use **, and** before c.

5. a. Annie learned English in school.
    b. Rose learned English in school.

NOTE: Use **and**.

6. a. They learned Romany from their mothers.
    b. They learned Romany from their fathers.
    c. They learned Romany from their neighbors.

NOTE: Use ..., ..., **and** ....

7. a. Today, not many people speak Romany.
    b. Today, not many people read Romany.
    c. Today, not many people write Romany.

NOTE: Use ..., ..., **or** ....

8. a. Annie is lucky.
    b. Rose is lucky.

NOTE: Use **and**.

9. a. They use English at work.
    b. They usually speak Romany to each other.
    c. They usually speak Romany with their friends.

NOTE: Use **, but** after a.
          Use **and** between b and c.

C. Reading Check

After reading the sentences in Part B, decide whether these statements are *True (T)* or *False (F). Circle the correct letter.*

T   F   1. Rose and Annie speak only English.

T   F   2. They are gypsies

T   F   3. They are from India.

T   F   4. They speak English at home.

T   F   5. They are lucky to know two languages.

T   F   6. Romany is a Romance language.

T   F   7. They learned English from their parents.

T   F   8. Today many people speak Romany.

D. Write Away

Combine the sentences in Part B. Follow the suggestions in the *NOTES.* Write each group as one sentence. Do NOT write the numbers. After you finish, check your work with your teacher.

E. Writing Follow-Up

Write a paragraph about your languages. The title is, "I'm Bilingual." Use the sentences that follow in your paragraph.

In Sentence 1 complete the missing information and combine these two sentences with **, and**:

My first language is ....
My second language is ....

In Sentence 2 complete the missing information:

I speak (*name of first language*) **with** (*whom?*)
(*where?*)

In Sentence 3, begin with **However,** and complete the missing information:

I speak (*name of second language*) **with** (*whom*)
(*where?*)

In Sentence 4, complete the missing information and combine these sentences with **, but**:

I learned (*name of first language*) (*where?*)
I learned (*name of second language*) (*where?*)

In Sentence 5, complete the missing information:

I feel (*how?*) **because I know two languages**.

I'm Bilingual

_____

_____

_____

_____

_____

_____

Unit 4

The Flu

A.   Vocabulary Preview

Match the following:

g   1. sneeze

_____ 2. cough

_____ 3. run

_____ 4. water

_____ 5. burn

_____ 6. rise

_____ 7. come down with

_____ 8. ache/hurt

_____ 9. sweat

a. an action in the nose if you have the flu

b. an action in the eyes if you have the flu

c. a feeling in the throat if you have the flu

d. an increase in body temperature

e. water through the skin when you are hot

f. an action in the throat and chest when you have the flu

g. sudden release of air through the mouth and nose

h. begin to get sick

i. feel pain

Circle the one word that is different in each group:

1.   sneezing   coughing   (hurting)

2.   aching   watering   hurting

3.   rising   running   watering

4.   burning   rising   sneezing

5.   sweating   watering   hurting

B.   Read the following:

The Flu

(1) I am sneezing a lot.   (2) I am coughing.   (3) My nose is running.   (4) My eyes are watering.   (5) My chest is hurting.   (6) My head is aching.   (7) My throat is burning.   (8) My temperature is rising.   (9) I am sweating.   (10) I am coming down with the flu.

C.   Reading Check

Find another way to say these sentences. Write them in the blanks.

1. I have a runny nose.   *My nose is running.*

2. I have watery eyes. _____

3. I have pain in my chest. _____

4. I have a headache. _____

5. There is a burning in my throat. _____

6. I am catching the flu. _____

7. I have a fever. _____

8. I am wet with sweat. _____

D.   Write Away

1.   You are in your doctor's office, and he is asking you questions. His first question is: **Are you sneezing a lot?** Rewrite the paragraph in Part B. What are his other questions?

NOTE: Do NOT rewrite (10).

2.   Now answer the questions the doctor asked in Exercise 1.

NOTE: Do NOT write (10).

Doctor's Question	Your Answer
Are you sneezing a lot?	**Yes, I am.**

3.   Another person in the doctor's office does NOT have the flu. Answer the doctor's questions in the *negative* for that person.

NOTE: Do NOT write (10).

The first answer is: **No, I'm not.**

4.   The next day you are feeling better. Rewrite the paragraph in Part B. Use contractions.

Your first sentence: **Today I'm not sneezing a lot.**

5.   Rewrite the paragraph to describe how someone usually feels when he or she is coming down with the flu.

NOTE: Do NOT rewrite (10).

Your first sentence: **He (or she) sneezes a lot.**

6.   Rewrite the paragraph to describe how you felt all day yesterday. Do NOT write the numbers.

Your first sentence: **All day yesterday I was sneezing a lot.**

7.   Rewrite the paragraph in Part B. Make the following changes. Use contractions when possible. Do NOT write the numbers.

Combine (1) and (2) with **and**. Write **coughing** before **a lot** in (1). Do NOT write **I am** in (2).
Combine (3) and (4) with **, and**.
After (5), write **, and I have a headache.** Do NOT write (6).
Do not change (7).
Write **Because** before (8), put a comma **,** after (8), and combine with (9).
Write **I think** before (10).

E.   Writing Follow-Up

Finish the following paragraph. Write at least six sentences.

My World

At this moment I'm looking around me. These things are happening. _____

_____

_____

_____

_____

_____

_____

Unit 5

Percy the Clown

A. Vocabulary Preview

In the paragraph in Part B, find another way to say the
following expressions. Write your verson of the expression in the blank.

| | |
| Expression | Sentence Number |

1. He doesn't have a job at the   (2)
    present time.

    He is not working now.

2. He is trying to find a job.   (3)

    _____

3. He has a positive attitude.   (4)

    _____

4. He is able to do the job.   (5)

    _____

5. Everyone knows his background.   (6)

    _____

6. He has a good sense of humor.   (7)

    _____

7. He is quick to learn, and people   (8) and (9)
    love him.

    _____

8. He is reliable and tells the truth.   (10) and (11)

    _____

B.   Read the following:

Percy the Clown

(1) Percy is a clown. (2) He is not working now. (3) He is looking for a job in a circus. (4) He is optimistic. (5) He is qualified. (6) Everybody is familiar with his qualifications. (7) He is funny. (8) He is intelligent. (9) He is lovable. (10) He is dependable. (11) He is honest. (12) He is dedicated. (13) His work is very important to him. (14) He is in love with the circus.

C.   Reading Check

After reading the paragraph in Part B, decide whether these statements are *True (T)* or *False (F)*. Circle the correct letter.

T   F   1. Percy is working in a circus.

T   F   2. He is an acrobat in the circus.

T   F   3. He has the right qualifications for the job.

T   F   4. He is positive.

T   F   5. He tells the truth.

T   F   6. All of Percy's qualifications are good.

T   F   7. Percy isn't dependable.

T   F   8. Percy likes the circus.

D.   Write Away

1.   Rewrite the paragraph in Part B. Use contractions.

Your first sentence: **Percy's a clown.**

2.   Lili has a magic act. Write about her.

Your first sentence: **Lili is a magician.**

3.   In (4), (5), (7), (8), (9), (10), (11), and (12) of the model paragraph, add **a(n) ... clown**. Use contractions.

Sentence (4) is: **He's an optimistic clown.**

4.   Rewrite the paragraph about Lili. In (4), (5), (7), (8), (9), (10), (11), and (12), add **a(n) ... magician**. Use contractions.

Sentence (4) is: **She's an optimistic magician.**

5.   You are Percy. Write about yourself.

Your first sentence: **I'm a clown.**

6.   You are the circus manager, and you are interviewing Percy for a job. Change each sentence in the paragraph to a question.

Your first question: **Are you a clown?**

NOTE: In (6), change **everybody** to **anybody**.

7. Rewrite the paragraph in Part B. Follow these instructions. Do NOT write the numbers.

Combine (1) and (2) with **, but**.
Combine (4) and (5) with **because**.
Do NOT change (6).
Combine (7) through (12) with ..., ..., ..., ..., ...,
  and ....
Combine (13) and (14) with **because**.

E.   Writing Follow-Up

Write a paragraph about someone's job (teacher, doctor, accountant, mechanic, electrician, etc.). Give your paragraph the title, "(Person's Name) the (name of job)." Include the following information in your paragraph.

Who is that person?
What is that person's job?
Is that person working now? If yes, where?
What are that person's qualifications?
Is that person's job important to him or her?
Is that person happy with his or her job?

Unit 6
Work, Work, and Play

A.   Vocabulary Preview

These words are in Part B. Match each word with its definition. (There is one definition that does not match any word.)

d 1. factory

_____ 2. operate

_____ 3. drive

_____ 4. relax

_____ 5. enjoy

_____ 6. collect

a. to work or make something work
b. to get happiness from things
c. to gather objects as a sport or a hobby
d. a building where goods are made, especially by machinery
e. to start; to take the first steps
f. to rest, to be less active
g. to control or direct the course of something

B.   Read the following:

Work, Work, and Play

(1) I work in a factory from Monday to Friday.   (2) I make shoes.   (3) I operate a sewing machine.   (4) My work day begins at 8 AM and ends at 4.   (5) After work I usually stop and buy a newspaper.   (6) Then I go home and have dinner.   (7) In the evening I drive a taxi.   (8) During the week I am very busy, but on the weekends I try to relax and enjoy my hobby.   (9) I collect stamps.

C. Reading Check

After reading the paragraph in Part B, decide whether these statements are *True (T)* or *False (F)*. Circle the correct letter.

T   F   1. I do not work in a factory on Saturday and Sunday.

T   F   2. I sew shoes by hand.

T   F   3. I work six hours each day.

T   F   4. I also have a job in the evening.

T   F   5. I'm a taxi driver on the weekends.

D. Write Away

1. My friend Hugo also works in a factory. Write about Hugo and me.

Your first sentence: **Hugo and I work in a factory from Monday to Friday.**

2. Hugo and Hector work together. Write about them.

Your first sentence: **Hugo and Hector work in a factory from Monday to Friday.**

3. Kate also works in a factory. Write about her.

Your first sentence: **Kate works in a factory from Monday to Friday.**

4. Five years ago I worked in a factory. Rewrite the paragraph in the *past tense.*

Your first sentence: **I worked in a factory five years ago.**

5. Read these sentences carefully.

Column A	Column B
I work in an office	I'm an office worker
I make dresses.	I'm a dressmaker.
I operate an elevator.	I'm an elevator operator.
He drives a truck.	He's a truck driver.
He collects coins.	He's a coin collector.

Now, rewrite the entire paragraph in Part B changing (1), (2), (3), (7), and (9) to sentences like those in Column B. Omit the numbers.

Your first two sentences: **I'm a factory worker from Monday to Friday. I'm a shoemaker.**

E. Writing Follow-Up

Select one of the following topics and write a paragraph.

1. Write about your job and your day by using the paragraph in Part B as a model.

2. Pretend that you are a journalist and interview someone about his or her job. Write a newspaper article about this person and what he/she does at work. Be sure to answer these questions in your article.

What is the person's job title?
What kind of work does he/she do?
Where does he/she work?
When does the person work?
What kind of hobby does he/she have?
Do you know any other interesting information about this person?

_____

_____

_____

_____

_____

_____

_____

_____

Unit 7

Early Morning Help

A.   Vocabulary Preview

Match the following:

*b*___ 1. trim   a. return
                                      b. cut neatly
___ 2. hedge   c. without care, quick
                                      d. isn't able to
___ 3. angry   e. a long row of trees or
                                         shrubs used as a fence
___ 4. belongs   f. not fully awake
        to both   g. upset, irritated,
        of them.   unpleasant
                                      h. they own (it) together
___ 5. pajamas,   i. neatly arranged (as
        bathrobe,   hair)
        slippers   j. morning or bedtime
                                         clothing
___ 6. combed

___ 7. half-asleep

___ 8. can't

___ 9. impatient

___ 10. go back

B.   Read the following:

Early Morning Help

1. a. It is 6:30 in the morning.
    b. Mr. Chavez is trimming the hedge.
    c. The hedge is between his house and Mr.Kelly's
        house.

NOTE: Use **, and** between a. and b. Use **that** in c. Do NOT
          write **The hedge.**

2. a. He is using an electric trimmer.
    b. It is making a lot of noise.

NOTE: Use **, which** after a. Do NOT write **It** in b.

3. a. Mr. Chavez is a little angry.
    b. Mr. Kelly isn't helping him.

NOTE: Use **because** after a.

4. a. The hedge belongs to both of them.
    b. They usually trim it together.

NOTE: Use **, and**.

5. a. After a few minutes, Mr. Kelly comes out of his back door.
    b. He is wearing his pajamas.
    c. He is wearing his bathrobe.
    d. He is wearing his slippers.

NOTE: Use a comma **,** after a. Use . . . , . . . , **and** . . . . in b., c., and d. Do NOT write **He is**.

6. a. His hair isn't combed.
    b. He seems half-asleep.

NOTE: Use **, and**.

7. a. He is carrying his hedge trimmers.
    b. They are under his arm.

NOTE: Do NOT write **They are**.

8. a. Mr. Chavez says, "Good morning."
   b. Mr. Kelly doesn't answer.

NOTE: Use **, but**.

9. a. Mr. Kelly works fast
   b. Mr. Chavez can't keep up with him.

NOTE: Use **so** before **fast**. Use **that** after **fast**.

10. a. A short time later, they finish the hedge.
    b. Mr. Chavez thanks Mr. Kelly.
    c. He thanks him for his help.

NOTE: Use **, and**. Do NOT write **He thanks him** in c.

11. a. Mr. Kelly answers.
    b. His answer is impatient.
    c. "You're welcome. Now I can go back to bed."

NOTE: Write **impatiently** before **answers**. Write a comma **,** after **answers**. Do NOT write b. Do NOT change c.

C.   Reading Check

After reading the sentences in Part B, decide whether these statements are *True (T)* or *False (F)*. Circle the correct letter.

T   F   1. It's early in the morning.

T   F   2. Mr. Kelly is in a hurry.

T   F   3. They work together.

T   F   4. Mr. Chavez seems half-asleep.

T   F   5. The hedge is behind their houses.

T   F   6. They finish their work within a few minutes.

T   F   7. They are wearing their pajamas.

T   F   8. Mr. Kelly finishes quickly because he wants to sleep.

D.   Write Away

1.   Combine the sentences in Part B. Follow the suggestions in the *NOTES*. Write each group as one sentence. Do NOT write the numbers. After you finish, check your work with your teacher.

2.   After you combine all the sentences, rewrite the paragraph. Change **Mr. Chavez** and **Mr. Kelly** to **Mrs. Chavez** and **Mrs. Kelly**.

Your first sentence: **It was 6:30 in the morning, and Mrs. Chavez was trimming the hedge between her house and Mrs. Kelly's house.**

E.   Writing Follow-Up

We all know a funny story or two about people. Write a story that you know. Use the actual words that the two people say. Write your own title at the top. Include the following information in your paragraph:

the time of the story
the names of the two people in the story
the appearance of these two people
the words these two people say
the funny part of the story

_____

_____

_____

_____

_____

_____

_____

_____

_____

Unit 8

The Concert

A. Vocabulary Preview

Match the following:

*b*____ 1. hurry

____ 2. buy

____ 3. ticket

____ 4. program

____ 5. usher

____ 6. relax

____ 7. Enjoy
       yourself.

a. a piece of paper that allows you into a concert or movie

b. speed it up

c. purchase, or give money for something

d. have a good time!

e. make yourself comfortable

f. a person who shows you your seat in a theater

g. a paper with the order of events in a play or concert

B.   Read the following:

The Concert

(1) Hurry. (2) Buy your ticket at the window. (3) Give it to the usher. (4) Get your program. (5) Find your seat quickly. (6) Be quiet. (7) Look at your program. (8) Listen to the music. (9) Relax and enjoy yourself.

C. Reading Check

What is the order of events? Write numbers.

_____ a. You pay for your ticket.

_____ b. You listen to the music.

_____ c. You are comfortable and enjoy yourself.

__1__ d. You are in a hurry to get to the concert.

_____ e. The usher takes your ticket.

_____ f. You are quiet.

_____ g. You read your program.

_____ h. You find your seat.

D. Write Away

1. We are together. Rewrite the paragraph in Part B with **Let's**.

Your first sentence: **Let's hurry**.

2. Mary likes concerts, but she is always late. Rewrite the paragraph.

Your first sentence: **Mary hurries to the concert.**

3. Helen and George went to the concert last night. Rewrite the paragraph.

Your first sentence: **Helen and George hurried to the concert**.

NOTE: Use **They** in (2) through (9).

4.   Rewrite the paragraph. Report what a friend told you to do.

Your first sentence: **She told us to hurry.**

6.   Report what a friend told Helen and George to do.

Your first sentence: **She told them to hurry.**

7.   You went to the concert last night. Write about yourself. Use the paragraph as a model. Do NOT write the numbers. Follow the directions below:

In (1), Write **First, . . . because I was late.**

Your first sentence: **First, I hurried because I was late.**

Before (2), write **Next, ...**
Before (3), write **Then, ...**
Combine (3) and (4) with **and**.
Before (5), write **After that, ...**
Combine (5) and (6) with **and**.
Before (7), write **Then, ...**
Before (8), write **Finally, ...**
Combine (8) and (9) with **and**.

E.   Writing Follow-Up

A friend is coming to your house. Write directions to
your house from the train station, bus station, or airport.
Use the verb forms in the paragraph and these words in
your instructions: *First, Then, After that, Finally.*

Directions to My House

_____

_____

_____

_____

_____

_____

_____

Unit 9

Did You Know That ... ?

A. Vocabulary Preview

These words are in Part B. Match each word with its definition. (There is one definition that does not match any word.)

___*d*___ 1. retired

_____ 2. curious

_____ 3. favorite

_____ 4. encyclopedia

_____ 5. dictionary

_____ 6. memory

_____ 7. remember

_____ 8. compare

_____ 9. skyscraper

a. the ability to remember information

b. a book that gives a list of words in alphabetical order, with their pronunciations and meanings

c. a very tall city building

d. no longer working, usually because of age

e. useless information or things

f. always wanting to know or learn more

g. a book or set of books with information

h. to keep in the memory

i. to point out the likeness or difference of people or things

j. liked more than anything else

B.   Read the following:

Did You Know That . . . ?

Despene is a retired math teacher. She reads every day and is curious about everything. Her favorite books are encyclopedias and dictionaries. She has a good memory. She remembers a lot of information, and she likes to compare it. Now, Despene wants you to compare this information about skyscrapers and bridges with her.

Skyscrapers	Number of Floors
World Trade Center	110
Empire State Building	102
Chrysler Building	77
One Chase Manhattan Plaza	60
Woolworth Building	60

Bridges	Length
The Verrazano-Narrows Bridge, New York	1298 m (4260 ft.)
The Golden Gate Bridge, San Francisco	1280 m (4200 ft.)
The Mackinac Bridge, Mackinac, Michigan	1158 m (3800 ft.)
The Kanmon Bridge, Japan	712.2 m (2336 ft.)
The Angostura Bridge, Venezuela	712.2 m (2336 ft.)

C.   Reading Check

After reading the paragraph in Part B, decide whether these statements are *True (T), False (F),* or *Probably True (PT).* Circle the correct letter.

T   F   PT   1. Despene is an intelligent woman.

T   F   PT   2. She worked as a math teacher for many years.

T   F   PT   3. She is not interested in facts.

T   F   PT   4. She finds a lot of information in certain kinds of books.

T   F   PT   5. When Despene reads, she likes to find similarities or differences in the information.

D.   Write Away

1.   Look at the information about skyscrapers. Then use these expressions to fill in the blanks in the paragraph that follows: *as tall as, taller than, the tallest.*

(1) There are many tall buildings in the world.   (2) People call them skyscrapers.   (3) There are many skyscrapers in New York City.   (4) For example, the World Trade Center is _the tallest_ building in New York City.   (5) The Empire State Building is not _____

_____ the World Trade Center.   (6) However, it is

_____ the Chrysler Building.   (7) One Chase

Manhattan Plaza is _____ the Woolworth

Building.   (8) Both of them have sixty floors.

2.   Look at the information about bridges. Then use
these expressions to fill in the blanks in the paragraph
that follows: _as long as, longer than, the longest._

   (1) There are many long suspension bridges in the

world.   (2) The Verrazano-Narrows Bridge in New York

City is _____ suspension bridge in North

America. (3) The Golden Gate Bridge is not _____

_____ the Verrazano-Narrows Bridge.   (4) However,

it is _____ the Mackinac Bridge.   (5) The

Kanmon Bridge is _____ the Angostura

Bridge.   (6) Both of them are 712.2 meters (2336 feet)

long.

3.   Use the paragraph in Exercise D.2. above as a model to compare millionaires and their wealth.

Millionaires	Wealth
J. Donnal Trumpet	$200 million
J. Paul Gritty	$175 million
A. Morito Soni	$150 million
King Ibn Ahmed	$100 million
Princess Serena	$100 million

Use these expressions: *as rich as, richer than, the richest.*

Your first sentence: **There are many millionaires in the world.**

4.   Use the paragraph in Exercise D.2. above as a model to compare these fast-running animals.

Animals	Speed, per hour
cheetah	113 km (70 mi.)
gazelle	100 km (66 mi.)
impala	80 km (50 mi.)
greyhound	64 km (40 mi.)
zebra	64 km (40 mi.)

Use these expressions: *as fast as, faster than, the fastest.*

Your first sentence: **There are many animals that run fast, but the cheetah is the fastest animal in the world.**

E.   Writing Follow-Up

Write a paragraph to compare some friends, relatives, teachers, or co-workers. These are some adjectives that you can use in your paragraph.

tall/short	pretty	quiet/loud (speaking
thin/heavy	neat	voice)
skinny/fat	smart	funny (in the sense of
old/young	lazy	making you laugh)
shy/friendly	rich	

_____

_____

_____

_____

_____

_____

_____

_____

Unit 10

Miriam's Routine

A. Vocabulary Preview

Find the sentence in Column B that is close in meaning to the sentence in Column A.

Column A	Column B

_d_ 1. Miriam cooks breakfast.

a. She sweeps the floor.

b. She is learning how to solve crimes and catch criminals.

_____ 2. She cleans the house.

_____ 3. She arrives at school before her class starts.

c. She has time to have a cup of tea and to relax.

_____ 4. She likes her classmates.

d. She makes a pot of coffee and some toast.

_____ 5. She wants to become a detective.

e. Her classmates are nice and friendly.

B.   Read the following:

Miriam's Routine

(1) Miriam cooks breakfast every morning. (2) After breakfast she washes the dishes and cleans the house. (3) She listens to the radio as she works. (4) When she finishes her housework, she walks to the bus stop. (5) She waits for the bus. (6) It usually arrives on time. (7) At school she rests before her class starts. (8) She has a cup of tea. (9) She relaxes. (10) She smiles because she likes her classmates. (11) Her classmates are all serious students. (12) Miriam studies at the Police Academy. (13) She wants to become a detective.

C.   Reading Check

After reading the paragraph in Part B, decide whether these statements are *True, False,* or *Probably.*

1.   Miriam is a busy woman. _____

2.   The bus is always on time. _____

3.   She is nervous before her _____

     class begins.

4.   Some of her classmates   _____

     are men.

5.   Her classmates are likable. _____

D.   Write Away

1.   Miriam and Joanne are classmates, and their daily routines are the same. Rewrite the paragraph in Part B and describe their routine.

Your first sentence: **Miriam and Joanne cook breakfast every morning**.

2.   Miriam's routine is different now. Describe her routine last year.

Your first sentence: **Last year Miriam cooked breakfast every morning**.

3.   Rewrite the paragraph in Part B by combining the following sentences. Omit the numbers.

Do NOT change (1), (2), and (3).
Combine (4) and (5) with **, where**.
Do NOT change (6) and (7).
Combine (8) and (9) with **and**.
Combine (10) and (11) with **, who**.

NOTE: Omit **Her classmates** in (11).

Combine (12) and (13) with **, and**.

E.   Writing Follow-Up

Write your daily routine on the days that you go to school
or to work.

_____

_____

_____

_____

_____

_____

_____

_____

Unit 11

Mama's Remedy

Mother's Chicken Soup
1 4 lb. chicken
4 chicken wings
1 clove of garlic
1 medium onion
2 carrots
2 stalks celery
½ bunch parsley
1 bay leaf
1½ teaspoon salt
½ teaspoon black pepper-
    corns
4 quarts cold water

1.

2.

3.

A.   Vocabulary Preview

Match the following:

*i*___ 1. catch a cold

___ 2. follow
someone's
advice

___ 3. bowl

___ 4. recipe

___ 5. breathe the
steam

___ 6. breathe deeply

___ 7. take a bath

___ 8. warm

___ 9. drink plenty
of liquids

___ 10. fever

___ 11. remedy

a. take a lot of milk,
juice, water, etc.
inside the body.
b. not cold
c. instructions for
making food
d. take in the
vapor from a hot
liquid, like soup
e. do what
someone suggests
f. a container for
soup or cereal
g. take in a lot of
air into the
chest
h. wash the body
i. get sick with
sneezing,
coughing, and fever
j. a hot feeling in
the body
k. a cure; a way to
make yourself feel
better when you
are sick

B.   Read the following:

Mama's Remedy

(1) I always catch a cold in the winter. (2) I know exactly what to do. (3) I follow my mother's advice. (4) I make a hot bowl of chicken soup. (5) I use her recipe. (6) There's something magic about my mother's chicken soup. (7) For a few minutes, I breathe the steam from the hot soup. (8) I breathe very deeply. (9) Then, I eat the soup slowly. (10) After that, I take a long, hot bath. (11) I go to bed. (12) I stay warm. (13) I drink plenty of liquids. (14) I take aspirin for the fever. (15) In a day or so, I feel OK again.

C.   Reading Check

Circle the correct words.

1. I always catch a (cold,   headache) in the (summer, winter).

2. I use my (mother's,   father's) advice to make (chicken,   vegetable) soup.

3. (After,   Before) I (breathe,   eat) the steam from the soup, I eat it (slowly,   quickly)

4. (Before,   After) I take a (hot,   cold) bath, I go to bed.

5. I drink (plenty,   a little bit) of (liquids,   aspirin) and take aspirin for the (cold,   fever).

6. I feel better in a few (days,   weeks).

D.   Write Away

1.   Write about Gretchen. She also has winter colds.

Your first sentence: **Gretchen always catches a cold in the winter.**

2.   Ken is another person who has a cold in the winter. Write about him.

Your first sentence: **Ken always catches a cold in the winter.**

3.   Fran and I also have winter colds. Write about us.

Your first sentence: **We always catch a cold in the winter.**

4.   Rewrite the paragraph. Do NOT write the numbers. Follow these suggestions.

Combine (1) and (2) with **, but**.
Do NOT change (3).
Combine (4) and (5). Write (5) first. In (5) write **Following her recipe,**. Do NOT write **I use**. Then, write (4).
Do NOT change (6).
Combine (7), (8), and (9). Write **very deeply** after (7). Do NOT write **I breathe** in (8). Write **, and** before (9).
Combine (10) and (11) with **and**.
Combine (12), (13), and (14) with **. . . , . . . , and . . . .**
Do NOT change (15).

E.   Writing Follow-Up

Write a paragraph about a remedy you know from your mother or grandmother. Write the title of your paragraph. Give this information in your paragraph:

The remedy (Is it for the flu? A bee sting? An upset stomach? A headache or backache? A burn?)
Whose remedy (Your mother's? Your grandmother's? Your father's? Your grandfather's?)
A description of the remedy (The preparations? The sequence? The results?)
The amount of time to use the remedy

_____

_____

_____

_____

_____

_____

_____

_____

Unit 12
Night Duty

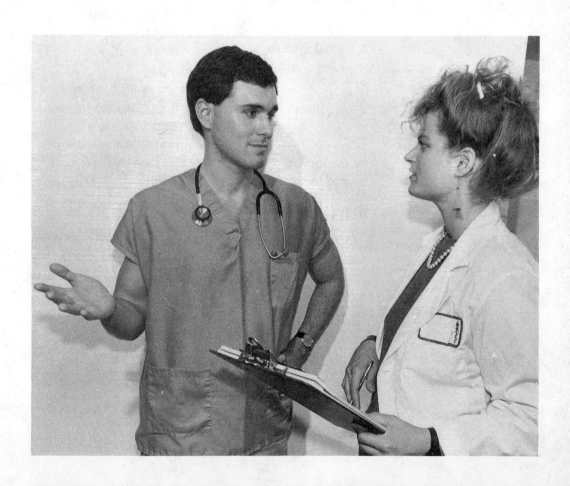

A. Vocabulary Preview

Match the following:

_i_   1. hospital

_____   2. go on duty

_____   3. patient

_____   4. check the patients' files

_____   5. head nurse

_____   6. tray

_____   7. take temperature

_____   8. cheer up someone

_____   9. back rub

_____ 10. get off duty

a. start one's job

b. stop one's job

c. a sick person

d. a flat holder for dishes

e. the supervising person who takes care of people in a hospital

f. make someone feel happy

g. a massage below the shoulders

h. read the sick people's reports

i. a place for sick people

j. measure the heat of the body

B.   Read the following:

Night Duty

1. a.   Maria goes to the hospital at 3:45 PM every day.
    b.   Jorge goes to the hospital at 3:45 PM every day.

NOTE: Use **Maria and Jorge**.

2. a.   She goes on duty at 4:00 PM.
    b.   He goes on duty at 4:00 PM.

NOTE: Use **he does, too**.

3. a.   They read the patients' names.
    b.   They check the files.
    c.   They get instructions from the head nurse.

NOTE: Use ..., ..., **and** ....

4. a.   At 6:00 PM Maria delivers dinner to the patients.
    b.   At 6:30 PM Jorge takes the dinner trays away.

NOTE: Use **, and**.

5. a.   Before the patients go to sleep, Maria takes the
         patients' temperatures.
    b.   Before the patients go to sleep, Jorge takes the
         patients' temperatures.

NOTE: Use **Maria and Jorge**.

6. a. Maria cheers up the lonely old lady in Room 315.
    b. Jorge gives a back rub to the gentleman in Room 316.

NOTE: Use **, and**.

7. a. Maria loves her work.
    b. Jorge loves his work.
    c. At midnight they are tired.
    d. At midnight they are ready to go home.

NOTE: Combine a. and b. with **Maria and Jorge**. Use **, but** before c. Use **and** between c. and d.

8. a. They say goodnight to the other nurses.
    b. They disappear into the night.

NOTE: Use **and**.

C. Reading Check

Match the following:

_____ 1. arrival at the
hospital

_____ 2. beginning of
duty

_____ 3. dinner time

_____ 4. remove trays

_____ 5. gives a patient
a back rub

_____ 6. end of duty

_____ 7. number of
hours they
work

_____ 8. cheers up a
patient

a. midnight
b. Jorge does this
after dinner
c. 3:45 PM
d. 4:00 PM
e. 6:00 PM
f. 6:30 PM
g. eight hours
h. Maria does this after
dinner

Cross out (X) the incorrect answer.

1. Maria and Jorge go to the hospital (every day,   at

3:45 PM,   at midnight).

2. When they go on duty, they (read the patients'

names,   take the patients' temperatures,

check the files).

3.   At midnight they (are tired,   are ready to go home,

go on duty).

4.   Before the patients go to sleep, Maria and Jorge (take

temperatures,   give a back rub,   cheer some-

one up,   deliver dinner).

5.   Maria and Jorge (love their work,   are glad to get

off duty,   work in a hospital,   work during

the morning).

D.   Write Away

Combine the sentences in Part B. Follow the suggestions
in the *NOTES*. Write each group as one sentence. Do
NOT write the numbers. After you finish, check your
work with your teacher.

E.   Writing Follow-Up

Write about your job. If you do not have a job, write about
your father's or your mother's job. Give your paragraph
a title, such as "My Job" or "My Father's Job." Include
the following information in your paragraph:

the time you go to your job
the time you start work
the first thing you do at work
the other things you do after that (Write at least three dif-
    ferent things you do at work.)
your feelings when it is time to leave work
your feelings about your job
the last thing you do at work

_____

_____

_____

_____

_____

_____

_____

_____

_____

Unit 13

The Morning Friend

A.   Vocabulary Preview

1.   Match the words that are opposite in meaning.

   C   1. famous

         2. happy

         3. early

         4. exciting
            and lively

         5. fast and
            loud

         6. current

         7. accurate

         8. helpful

         9. easy

         10. enjoyable

a. slow and soft
b. painful
c. unknown
d. dull and boring
e. old; out-of-date
f. late
g. wrong; incorrect
h. sad
i. unhelpful
j. difficult

2.   **Match these words with their meanings.**

___*d*___ 1. announcer

_____ 2. news

_____ 3. weather forecast

_____ 4. announcements

_____ 5. commercials

a. a description of future temperature and climatic conditions (rain, sun, snow, wind, etc.)

b. happenings from all over the world on radio, on TV, or in newspapers

c. kinds of news about public happenings like meetings or other news helpful to a group of radio listeners or TV viewers

d. a speaker on a radio or TV program

e. advertisements to help sell something on the radio or TV

B.   Read the following:

The Morning Friend

(1) Carlos is famous.   (2) He is a popular radio announcer.   (3) His program is on the radio early in the morning.   (4) It is exciting and lively.   (5) His music is fast and loud. (6) The news on his program is current.   (7) His weather forecast is accurate.   (8) His announcements are helpful.   (9) His commercials are funny.   (10) His voice is pleasant and happy.   (11) He is a friend to many people.   (12) His program is easy for him, and his work is enjoyable.

C.   Reading Check

Connect the adjectives to the nouns they describe. One noun is to be used three times.

Adjectives	Nouns
a. popular	radio announcer
b. early	work
c. exciting and lively	program
d. fast and loud	news
e. current	voice
f. accurate	commercials
g. helpful	announcements
h. funny	weather forecast
i. pleasant and happy	Carlos
j. easy	music
k. enjoyable	
l. famous	

D.   Write Away

1.   Nancy is also a radio announcer. Write about her.

Your first sentence: **Nancy is famous**.

2.   Jaime is a radio announcer who works at night. He is exactly the opposite of Carlos. Write about him.

Your first sentence: **Jaime is not famous**.

3.   Marcello is ten years old and a dreamer. Write about him.

Your first sentence: **Someday Marcello is going to be famous**.

4.   Carlos is now retired. Write about him in the past tense.

Your first sentence: **Forty years ago Carlos was famous**.

5.   Rewrite the paragraph in Part B. Omit the numbers. Follow the instructions below:

Do NOT change (1) and (2).
Write **exciting and lively** before **program** in (3). Do
      NOT write **it is** in (4).
Combine (5) and (6) with **, and**.
Combine (7), (8), and (9) with ..., ..., **and** ....
Write **Because** before and a comma (,) after (10). After
      the comma (,) in (10), write (11).
Do NOT change (12).

E.   Writing Follow-Up

Write a paragraph about a famous TV or radio personality, like Carlos, that you know. Give the paragraph the title, "My Favorite Radio (or TV) Personality." Include the following information:

when the program is on radio or TV
a description of the program
a description of the announcer's voice and personality
a description of the music on the program
a description of the news and weather forecast on the program
a description of the announcements and commercials on the program
a description of the announcer's feelings about his/ her work

_____

_____

_____

_____

_____

_____

_____

_____

_____

_____

Unit 14

Helmut Learns a Lesson

A. Vocabulary Preview

Match each word with its definition. (There is one definition that does not match any word.)

*h*___ 1. spoiled (adj.)

___ 2. worry

___ 3. food

___ 4. snack

___ 5. refuse

___ 6. beg

___ 7. increase

___ 8. greedily

a. ask with deep
   feeling
b. a small amount of
   food eaten between
   meals
c. a way of eating
   something quickly
   and selfishly
d. a flat piece of meat
e. cause anxiety or
   trouble
f. become greater in
   amount
g. something taken into
   the body to live
h. selfish from having
   too much attention
i. say no; not to do,
   give, or accept

B.   Read the following:

Helmut Learns a Lesson

1.   a.   Helmut is a teenager.
     b.   He is spoiled.
     c.   He does not like certain foods.

NOTE: Insert **spoiled** in b. in front of **teenager**. Use
          , who after a. Do NOT write **He is** in b. or
          He in c.

2.   a.   His mother often worries about his health.
     b.   She is a good cook.

NOTE: Use **, who** after **mother** and **is a good cook,**
          from b. Do NOT write **She** in b.

3.   a.   She always cooks good food.
     b.   Helmut won't eat her good food.

NOTE: Use **but** after a. Do NOT write **her good food** in
          b. Add **it** after **eat** in b.

4.   a.   One day Helmut and his parents are driving to
          their cabin.
     b.   The cabin is in the mountains.

NOTE: Do NOT write **The cabin is** in b.

5.   a.   On the way they stop for a snack.
     b.   Helmut refuses to eat.

NOTE: Use **, but** after a.

6. a. His mother begs him to eat a steak sandwich.
    b. She made the sandwich for him.

NOTE: Use **, which** after a. Do NOT write **the sandwich**
         in b.

7. a. Helmut won't eat it.
    b. It is cold.

NOTE: *Use* **because** *after a.*

8. a. He gets angry.
    b. He runs away into the forest.

NOTE: Use **and** after a. Do NOT write **He** in b.

9. a. A half-hour later, he decides to return to his
        parents.
    b. They are waiting for him in the car.

NOTE: Use **, who** after a. Omit **They** in b.

10. a. He cannot find the way.
     b. The way leads out of the forest.

NOTE: Use **that** after a. Do NOT write **The way** in b.

11. a. He is lost.
     b. He is frightened.
     c. He is hungry.

NOTE: Use **. . . , . . . , and** . . . . Do NOT write **He is** in b.
         and c.

12.   a.   It soon gets dark.
      b.   His fear increases.
      c.   His hunger increases.

NOTE: Use **, and** after a. Use **and** between b. and c.

13.   a.   He sees a dim light.
      b.   The light is shining in the darkness.

NOTE: Do NOT write **The light is** in b.

14.   a.   The light is coming from an old cabin.
      b.   The cabin is unpainted.
      c.   The cabin is near a stream.

NOTE: Insert **unpainted** in front of **cabin** in a. Do NOT
          write **The cabin is** in b. and c.

15.   a.   Helmut knocks on the door.
      b.   A poor woodcutter opens it.

NOTE: Use **, and** after a.

16.   a.   Helmut asks for some food.
      b.   The woodcutter only has some old bread.

NOTE: Use **, but** after a.

17.   a.   Helmut takes the old bread.
      b.   Helmut eats it greedily.

NOTE: Use **and** after a. Do NOT write **Helmut** in b.

18. a. The bread tastes delicious.
     b. It is not like his mother's good cooking.

NOTE: Use **, but** after a.

19. However, to a hungry person, old bread is as good
     as cake.

C. Reading Check

After reading the sentences in Part B, decide whether
these statements are *True (T) or False (F)*. Circle the correct letter.

T   F   1. Helmut likes to eat all kinds of food.

T   F   2. His mother does not prepare good food
                for him to eat.

T   F   3. Helmut does not like cold steak
                sandwiches.

T   T   4. He ran into the forest because he didn't
                like the snack his mother prepared.

T   F   5. Helmut knew how to find his way out of
                the forest.

T   F   6. He ate old bread because he was
                very hungry.

D. Write Away

1.   Combine the sentences in Part B. Follow the suggestions in the *NOTES.* Write each group as one sentence. Do NOT write the numbers. After you finish, check your work with your teacher.

2.   Write Helmut's story to a friend. Use the *past tense.*

Your first sentence: **Helmut was a spoiled teenager who did not like certain foods.**

E. Writing Follow-Up

Do you know a difficult or spoiled person? Write about him/her. Describe that person's difficult personality, his/her way of dealing with other people, how other people react to that person, and an incident when that person learned a lesson.

_____

_____

_____

_____

_____

_____

_____

_____

Unit 15

Waiting in the Rain

A.   Vocabulary Preview

Choose one of the words below to replace the underlined words or expressions in the paragraph that follows:

calmly	*hurry*	*smile*	*join*	*catch*
rush	*taxis*	*grab*	*push*	*argue*

Most   (1) ~~cabs~~ *taxis* in New York are yellow, and it is not easy to   (2) get one in bad weather. People often start to   (3) discuss emotionally if they all   (4) hurry to get into the same taxi. Everybody seems to be in such a (5) rush. They are not always kind to each other. They rarely   (6) show happiness by moving the ends of the lips upward. They sometimes   (7) use their arms to move each other. Sometimes people get so upset that they   (8) take in their hand each other's clothing. When it's raining in New York, it's best to   (9) become part of a group and wait. When others start to argue, you   (10) in a peaceful manner get into the taxi and ride away.

B.   Read the following:

Waiting in the Rain

1. a.   A tall man is waiting for a taxi.
    b.   A short man is waiting for a taxi.
    c.   They are waiting on the same corner.

NOTE: Write **and** between a. and b. Do NOT write **They are waiting** in c.

2. a.   An old woman joins them on the corner.
    b.   She also wants to catch a taxi.

NOTE: After a. write **because** and b.

3. a.   It is raining hard.
    b.   All the taxis pass without stopping.

NOTE: After a. write **, and** and b.

4. a.   Finally, a taxi stops.
    b.   The tall man rushes ahead of the short man.

NOTE: After a. write **, and** and b.

5. a.   The short man stops him.
    b.   They start to argue.

NOTE: After a. write **, and** and b.

6. a.   The tall man is in a hurry.
    b.   The short man was on the corner first.

NOTE: After a. write **, but** and b.

7. a.   The short man pushes the tall man.
    b.   The tall man grabs the short man's coat.

NOTE: After a. write **, and** and b.

8. a.   The old woman agrees with the tall man.
    b.   She also agrees with the short man.

NOTE: After a. write **, but** and b.

9. a.   The old woman calmly closes her umbrella.
    b.   She opens the taxi door.
    c.   She gets in the taxi.

NOTE: Combine a., b., and c. with ..., ..., **and** ....

10. a.   The taxi driver smiles.
     b.   He drives away.

NOTE: Write **and** after a. Do NOT write **He** in b.

C. Reading Check

After reading the sentences in Part B, decide whether these statements are *True (T)*, *False (F)*, or *Unknown (U)*. Circle the correct letter.

T   F   U   1. Three people are waiting on the corner.

T   F   U   2. They are waiting for a bus.

T   F   U   3. It is difficult to catch a taxi because of the rain.

T   F   U   4. The old woman argues with the two men.

T   F   U   5. The men are in a hurry

T   F   U   6. The men want to be nice to the old woman, and they give her the taxi.

T   F   U   7. The taxi driver wants the old woman to get into the taxi.

D. Write Away

Combine the sentences in Part B. Follow the suggestions in the *NOTES*. Write each group as one sentence. Do NOT write the numbers. After you finish, check your work with your teacher.

E.   Writing Follow-Up

Rewrite this story from the old woman's point of view.
Change to the *past tense*.

_____

_____

_____

_____

_____

_____

_____

Unit 16

Happy Birthday, Masako

A. Vocabulary Preview

1. Match these verbs with their meanings.

_____*h*_ 1. put	a. say in a loud voice
_____ 2. light	b. express joy with loud, explosive sounds through the mouth
_____ 3. get ready	
_____ 4. pour	c. stop electricity
_____ 5. spill	d. drop water or other liquid
_____ 6. turn off	e. transfer water or other liquid from one container to another
_____ 7. laugh	f. prepare yourself
_____ 8. shout	g. start a fire with a match
	h. place something somewhere

2. Cross out (X) the one word that is different in each group.

1. pour   spill   tu~~rn~~ off

2. anniversary   wedding   retirement   birthday   funeral

3. champagne   beer   soda   music   cake

4. cake   cookies   potato chips   soda

B. Read the following:

Happy Birthday, Masako

(1) Be quiet.   (2) Get ready.   (3) Put the cake on the table.   (4) Light the candles.   (5) Open the bottle.   (6) Pour the champagne.   (7) Don't spill it.   (8) Turn off the record player. (9) Turn off the light. (10) Don't laugh.   (11) Shout, "Happy Birthday, Masako."

C. Reading Check

After reading the sentences in Part B, decide whether these statements are *True (T)*, *False (F)*, or *Unknown (U)*. Circle the correct letter.

T   F   U   1. It's an anniversary party.

T   F   U   2. The party is a surprise

T   F   U   3. The party is for Masako.

T   F   U   4. Masako knows about the party in the beginning.

T   F   U   5. They have refreshments at the party.

T   F   U   6. They have Japanese music at the party.

T   F   U   7. They spill the champagne.

T   F   U   8. They turn off the music and the lights.

D. Write Away

1. We are together. Rewrite the paragraph with **Let's**.

Your first sentence: **Let's be quiet.**

NOTE: In (7) write **Let's not spill it**. (10) is like (7).

2. We are planning a surprise birthday party for Masako. Tell what we are **going to** do or **not going to** do.

Your first sentence: **We're going to be quiet.**

3. Tell what we must do for Masako's party.

Your first sentence: **We must be quiet.**

4. Masako's party was last night. Tell what we did.

Your first sentence: **We were quiet.**

5. Rewrite the paragraph as if it happened yesterday. Do NOT write the numbers. Follow the suggestions below:

Your first sentence: **First, we were quiet.**

In (2), write **Next,** ....
In (3), write **Then,** ....
In (4), write **After that,** ....
In (5), write **Then,** .... Combine (5) with (6) with **and**.
Change (7) to past tense.
In (8), write **Afterwards,** .... Combine (8) and (9) with **and**.
Change (10) to past tense.
In (11), write **Finally,** ....

E.   Writing Follow-Up

In a paragraph describe the last party you attended. Give the paragraph the title, "A Good Party." Include the following information:

the preparations before the party (Who planned it?)
the location of the party (Where was it?)
the occasion for the party (Birthday? Anniversary?
    Wedding? Retirement? Surprise?)
the refreshments at the party (Food and drink?)
the events at the party (What happened? Music? Games?)
the ending of the party (Time?)

_____

_____

_____

_____

_____

_____

_____

_____

Unit 17

The TV Star

A.   Vocabulary Preview

Match the following:

*h*____   1. performer

____   2. extraordinary

____   3. particularly

____   4. freshness

____   5. variety

____   6. humor

____   7. stylish

____   8. star

____   9. talented

a. a famous performer
b. newness; vitality
c. comedy
d. in the latest fashion
e. many different activities
f. very
g. very unusual
h. an actor or singer on TV
i. able to do a lot of different things, like singing and acting

B.   Read the following:

The TV Star

1. a. She is a television performer.
    b. She is extraordinary.

NOTE: Write **extraordinary** before **television performer** in a. Do NOT write **she is** in b.

2. a. Many people watch her program.
    b. The program is musical.
    c. The program is on TV every week.

NOTE: Use **musical** before **program** in a. Do NOT write **The program is** in b. After a., use **on TV every week**. Do NOT write **The program is** in c.

3. a. She is not really beautiful.
    b. She is not particularly talented.
    c. Her face is famous.
    d. Her body is famous.
    e. Her voice is famous.

NOTE: In a. and b. write **nor** after **beautiful** and before **particularly talented**. Do NOT write **She is not** in b. Combine b. and c. with **, but**. Combine c., d., and e. with **..., ..., and ....**

4. a. People like the freshness of her show.
    b. People like the humor of her show.
    c. People like the variety of her show.

NOTE: Combine a., b., and c. with **..., ..., and ....**

5. a. She sings at the opening of the program.
    b. She sings at the closing of the program.

NOTE: Write **and**.

6. a. She always wears a dress.
    b. The dress is stylish.

NOTE: Write **stylish** before **dress** in a. Do NOT write **The dress is** in b.

7. a. She speaks to the audience
    b. Her speech is soft.

NOTE: Write **softly** after speaks in a. Do NOT write **Her speech is** in b.

8. a. This young woman is a daughter to every
        father and mother.
    b. This young woman is a sister to every woman.
    c. This young woman is a lover to every young
        man.

NOTE: Combine a., b., and c. with . . . , . . . , **and** . . . .

9. a. Each person sees her in a different manner.
    b. To all, she is a star.

NOTE: Combine a. and b. with **, and**.

C. Reading Check

After reading the sentences in Part B, decide whether
these statements are *True (T), False (F),* or *Unknown (U).*
Circle the correct letter.

T   F   U   1. The TV star is very beautiful.

T   F   U   2. She is a very talented performer.

T   F   U   3. She dresses very stylishly.

T   F   U   4. Her show is a variety show.

T   F   U   5. She is a good dancer.

T   F   U   6. She is a musical performer.

D.   Write Away

1.   Combine the sentences in Part B. Follow the suggestions in the *NOTES.* Write each group as one sentence. Do NOT write the numbers. After you finish, check your work with your teacher.

2.   Rewrite the paragraph in Exercise 1 above. Write about Clint Sellek, who is also an extraordinary performer. Make the changes below:

Your first sentence: **Clint is an extraordinary television performer**.

In (2): His show is a **detective** program.
In (3): He is not **so handsome**.
In (4): His show has **adventure, romance,** and **excitement**.
In (5): He **speaks** at the beginning and end of the show.
In (6): He wears a **suit**.
In (7): His speech is **sincere**.
In (8): Change **woman** to **man, daughter** to **son** in a. Change **sister** to **brother, woman** to **man** in b. Change **man** to **woman** in c.
In (9): Change pronouns.

E.   Writing Follow-Up

Write a paragraph about your favorite television performer. Write the title "My favorite TV Star," or write the
person's name in the title. Include the following information in your paragraph:

*His or her TV program (What kind of program is it? How
    often is it on TV? Why do you like the program? What
    is the opening and closing of the program?)*
*His or her appearance (Is (s)he beautiful/handsome?
    Color of hair? Color of eyes? Tall or short? Kind
    of clothing?)*
His or her talent (Singer? Dancer? Actor? Comedian?)
Manner of speaking (Loudly? Softly? Quickly? Slowly?)
How people see this performer

_____

_____

_____

_____

_____

_____

_____

_____

Unit 18

High Blood Pressure

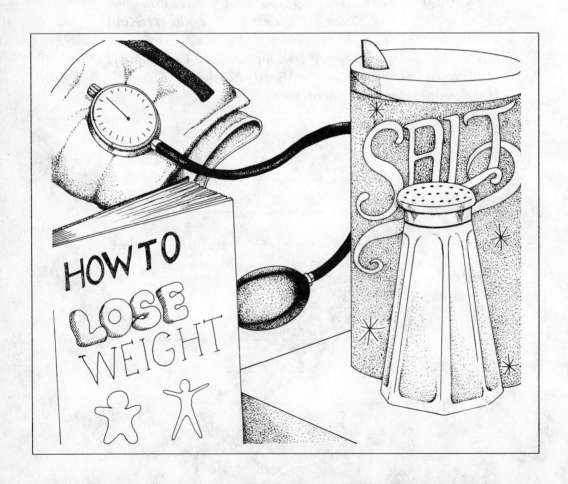

A.   Vocabulary Preview

Match the following:

_**c**_ 1. hypertension

_____ 2. *watch* (one's weight)

_____ 3. worried

_____ 4. exercise

_____ 5. prescribe

_____ 6. remember

_____ 7. high blood pressure

a. be careful about

b. physical activity like running, walking, swimming

c. another name for high blood pressure

d. give instructions for the use of medicine

e. call back into the mind

f. preoccupied; concerned about very much

g. a sickness that involves tension in the blood vessels of the body

B.   Read the following:

High Blood Pressure

(1) Mr. Petrosky has high blood pressure. (2) His doctor calls it hypertension. (3) Mr. Petrosky watches his weight and his diet. (4) He doesn't use salt on his food. (5) He exercises an hour each day. (6) Mr. Petrosky isn't worried. (7) His doctor prescribes medicine for him. (8) He remembers to take his medicine every day.

C. Reading Check

Choose the words to complete the following sentences.
Some sentences have more than one correct answer.

_____ 1. Mr. Petrosky's
          name for his
          sickness is . . . .

_____ 2. His doctor's name
          for the sickness
          is . . . .

_____ 3. Mr. Petrosky is
          careful about his
          . . . .

_____ 4. He eats his food
          without . . . .

_____ 5. Each day Mr.
          Petrosky . . . .

_____ 6. Mr. Petrosky's
          feeling about his
          sickness is that
          . . . .

_____ 7. His doctor's
          prescription is for
          . . . .

a. exercises
b. he isn't worried
c. weight
d. hypertension
e. salt
f. high blood
   pressure
g. diet
h. takes his
   medicine
i. medicine

D.   Write Away

1. Mr. Petrosky's wife also has hypertension. Write about her.

Your first sentence: **Mrs. Petrosky has high blood pressure.**

2. Now write about Mr. and Mrs. Petrosky.

Your first sentence: **Mr. and Mrs. Petrosky have high blood pressure.**

3. Pretend you have high blood pressure. Write about yourself.

Your first sentence: **I have high blood pressure.**

4. Now Mr. Petrosky's blood pressure is down. He is better. Write about it.

Your first sentence: **Mr. Petrosky had high blood pressure.**

5. Insert the following words in the paragraph.

In (1), **slightly** before **high**
In (3), **carefully** before **watches**
In (4), **any** before **salt**
In (5), **always** before **exercises**
In (6), **very** before **worried**
In (7), **family** before **doctor** and **proper** before
    medicine
In (8), **usually** before **remembers**

6. **Rewrite the paragraph in Exercise 5 above. Do NOT write the numbers. Follow these suggestions:**

Combine (1) and (2) with **, but**.
Combine (3) and (4) with **, and**.
Do NOT change (5).
Combine (6) and (7) with **because**.
Combine (8) and (9) with **, which**. Do NOT write **his medicine** in (8).

E.   Writing Follow-Up

Write a paragraph about a health problem and what you can do to stay healthy. Give your paragraph a title. Include the following information:

What is the health problem? (High blood pressure? Diabetes? Back problems? Tension and anxiety?)
What do you do about the problem? (What do you eat? What don't you eat?)
What do you do each day? (Exercise? Relax? Meditate? Take medicine?)
What does your doctor say about the problem?

_____

_____

_____

_____

_____

_____

_____

Unit 19
An Irish Story

A.   Vocabulary Preview

Match the following:

_a_	1. leprechaun	a. a small person in Irish mythology
_____	2. mysterious	b. follow through or do as one said
_____	3. sly and clever	c. a place with a lot of trees
_____	4. cries	d. a metal container
_____	5. heavy	e. not light; hard to move
_____	6. pot	f. a cloth for wiping one's face
_____	7. handkerchief	g. a tool for moving dirt
_____	8. shovel	h. unknown, unexplainable
_____	9. keep a promise	i. tricky and untrustworthy like a fox
_____	10. forest	j. a person who kills animals
_____	11. hunter	k. shouts

B.   Read the following:

An Irish Story

1. a.   Leprechauns live in forests.
   b.   The forests are in Ireland.

NOTE: Write **in Ireland** at the end of a. Do NOT write
the rest of b.

2. a.   They have power.
   b.   Their power is mysterious.

NOTE: Write **mysterious** before **power** in a. Do NOT
write the rest of b.

3. a.   They are also sly.
   b.   They are also clever.

NOTE: Write **and**.

4. a.   One day a leprechaun catches his foot under
a rock.
   b.   He isn't able to move.

NOTE: Write **and**.

5. a.   A hunter hears his cries.
   b.   He goes to help.

NOTE: Write **and**.

6. a. The leprechaun promises the hunter a pot of gold.
    b. The hunter will move the rock.
    c. The hunter will free the leprechaun.

NOTE: Combine a. and b. with **if**. Write **and** between b. and c. Do NOT write **The hunter** in b. and c. Do NOT write **will** in c.

7. a. The hunter works very hard.
    b. He wants to move the stone.
    c. The stone is heavy.

NOTE: Do NOT write **He wants** in b. Write **heavy** before **stone** in b. Do NOT write **The stone is** in c.

8. a. At last, he frees the leprechaun.
    b. The leprechaun points to a tree.
    c. The tree is nearby.

NOTE: Write **, who** after a. Do NOT write **The leprechaun** in b. Write **nearby** before **tree** in b. Do NOT write **The tree is** in c.

9. a. The hunter ties his handkerchief around the tree.
    b. He tells the leprechaun not to remove it.

NOTE: Write **and**. Do NOT write **He** in b.

10. a. The leprechaun gives his promise.
     b. The hunter returns to his house.
     c. He returns to get a shovel.

NOTE: Write **, and** between a. and b. Do NOT write **He returns** in c.

11. a. He rushes back to the forest with his shovel.
    b. He tries to find the tree.
    c. The tree has the handkerchief around it.

NOTE: Write **and** between a. and b. Do NOT write **he** in
         b. Write **that** after b. Do NOT write **The tree**
         in c.

12. a. The hunter doesn't see the leprechaun.
    b. He sees something else.
    c. It makes him very unhappy.

NOTE: Write **, but** between a. and b. Write **that** after b.
         Do NOT write **It** in c.

13. a. Every tree in the forest has a handkerchief.
    b. The handkerchief is around it.

NOTE: Do NOT write **The handkerchief is** in b.

14. a. The leprechaun kept his word.
    b. The leprechaun was sly.

NOTE: Write **sly** before **leprechaun** in a. Do NOT write
         The leprechaun was in b.

C. Reading Check

After reading the sentences in Part B, decide whether these statements are *True (T)*, *False (F)*, or *Unknown (U)*. Circle the correct letter.

T   F   U   1. Leprechauns are mythical animals.

T   F   U   2. They have mysterious powers to move rocks.

T   F   U   3. The leprechaun gives the hunter a pot of gold.

T   F   U   4. The hunter knows the leprechaun is sly.

T   F   U   5. The leprechaun ties a handkerchief around the tree with the pot of gold.

T   F   U   6. The hunter rushes back to his house to get a handkerchief.

T   F   U   7. The leprechaun helps the hunter find the pot of gold.

T   F   U   8. The hunter finds the pot of gold.

D.   Write Away

1.   Combine the sentences in Part B. Follow the suggestions in the *NOTES.* Write each group as one sentence. Do NOT write the numbers. After you finish, check your work with your teacher.

2.   Rewrite the paragraph in Exercise 1 above. Tell the story from the leprechaun's point of view.

Your first sentence: **I live in a forest in Ireland.**

E.   Writing Follow-Up

Do you know a folk hero or a mythological story from your country? Write it below. Write your own title to the story. Answer these questions in your paragraph.

Who are the characters?
Where does the story take place?
What happens first?
What happens second?
What happens then?
What happens next?
What happens after that?
What happens finally?

Unit 20

My Brother and I

A.   Vocabulary Preview

Cross out (X) one word that is different in each group.

1.   old   tall   dark   ~~hair~~

2.   brother   athlete   heavy   hair

3.   have   better   eat   love

4.   friend   exercise   brother   athlete

5.   older   taller   darker   serious

6.   darker   older   better   taller

B.   Read the following:

My Brother and I

(1) I have an older brother. (2) His name is Ervin. (3) Ervin is six years older than I am. (4) We aren't much alike. (5) He's taller than I am. (6) His hair is darker than mine. (7) He's a better athlete. (8) I'm a better student than he is. (9) I'm heavier than he is. (10) I eat more than he does. (11) I get less exercise than he does. (12) I'm probably more serious than he is. (13) We both love a good laugh. (14) He's a great joke teller — much better than I am. (15) He's a good brother. (16) He's a good friend.

C.   Reading Check

Circle the correct answer. Then, say it.

1. Who is older?   My brother   I

2. Who is a better
    student?   My brother   I

3. Who is more athletic?   My brother   I

4. Who is heavier?   My brother   I

5. Who is darker?   My brother   I

6. Who eats less?   My brother   I

7. Who gets less
    exercise?   My brother   I

8. Who is more serious?   My brother   I

D.   Write Away

1.   As you can see in the chart below, the person who wrote the paragraph in Part B is Dan. Dan also has a sister, Rhoda. She's younger (by two years), shorter, a better tennis player, and a better student than Dan is. She also has curlier hair. Write about *her* from Dan's point of view. Use the *first person (I)*.

Your first sentence: **I have a younger sister.**

The Anderson Children

Characteristic	Dan	Bertha	Rhoda	Ervin
Age	18	20	16	24
Height (feet)	6	5'4"	5'3"	6'2"
(meters)	1.8	1.63	1.60	1.88
Weight (pounds)	180	120	125	210
(kilograms)	81.8	54.5	56.8	95.5
Hair Color	light brown straight	blond short	black curly	brown wavy
Athletic ability	poor	very good	excellent	good
Frequency of exercise each week	once	three times	two times	three times
Academic ability	good	good	excellent	very good

2. Write about the person (Dan) who wrote the paragraph. This time, tell the story in the *third person.*

Your first sentence: **Dan has an older brother.**

3. The chart has some information about Dan's brothers and sisters. Write about Ervin and Bertha.

Your first sentence: **Ervin has a younger sister.**

4. Write about the brothers, Ervin and Dan. Use the information from the chart.

Your first sentence: **Ervin has a younger brother.**

5. Write about the sisters, Bertha and Rhoda. Use the information from the chart.

Your first sentence: **Bertha has a younger sister.**

6.   Rewrite the paragraph. Follow these suggestions:

Combine (1), (2), and (3). After **brother**, write , **Ervin,**
   who and the rest of (3).

NOTE: Do NOT write **His name is** in (2) and **Ervin**
   in (3).

Do NOT change (4).
Combine (5) and (6) with , **and.**
In (7), write **also** after **He's.**
Before (8), write **However,.**
Combine (9), (10), and (11): (9) and (10) with **because**
   and (10) and (11) with , **and.**
Combine (12) and (13) with , **but.**
Before (14), write **As a matter of fact,.**
Combine (15) and (16): Write **not only** before **a good**
   brother in (15) and a semicolon (;) after (15). Write
   also before **a good friend** in (16).

E.   Writing Follow-Up

Write about yourself and a brother or sister. If you do not have a sister or brother, compare yourself with a friend. Give your paragraph a title like "My Sister (Brother, Friend) and I." Include the following information in your paragraph:

What is the name of your brother, sister, or friend?
Is that person younger or older?
Are you alike or unalike?
Is that person taller or shorter than you?
Is that person's hair darker or lighter than yours?
Is that person a better or a worse athlete than you? A better or a worse student than you?
Are you heavier or lighter than that person? Why?
Who is more serious?
How do you feel about that person?

_____

_____

_____

_____

_____

_____

_____

Unit 21

The Meeting

A. Vocabulary Preview

Match the following:

___*c*___ 1. attractive

_____ 2. refuse

_____ 3. polite

_____ 4. very few

_____ 5. middle-aged

_____ 6. romantic

_____ 7. notice

_____ 8. celebrate

_____ 9. anniversary

a. yearly celebration of marriage
b. have a good time
c. pretty (for a woman)
d. courteous, with good manners
e. look at
f. in a loving manner
g. not many
h. between 40 and 55 years old
i. say no

B. Read the following:

The Meeting

1. a. A woman is standing on the corner.
    b. She is attractive.
    c. She is young.

NOTE: Write **attractive, young** in a.

2. a. A man starts to talk to her.
    b. He is handsome.
    c. He is young.

NOTE: Write **handsome, young** in a.

3. a. He asks her to have dinner with him.
     b. She refuses.
     c. Her refusal is polite.

NOTE: Write **, but** between a. and b. Write **politely** in b.
        Do NOT write **her refusal is** in c.

4. a. Then, he invites her to have a cup of coffee.
     b. He wants to get to know her.

NOTE: Write **because** before b.

5. a. Again the young woman refuses.
     b. Her refusal is polite.
     c. She tells him to go away.

NOTE: See 3 above. Use **and** before c.

6. a. The young man is surprised.
     b. His surprise is complete.
     c. Very few women refuse to go out with him.

NOTE: See 3 above. Use **because** before c.

7. a. He begins to walk away.
     b. A short man walks toward the woman.
     c. The man is middle-aged.

NOTE: Use **As** before a. Write **middle-aged** in b. Do
        NOT write **The man is** in c.

8. a. The short man says "hello" to the young
        woman.
     b. He looks at her.
     c. His look is romantic.

NOTE: Use **and** between a. and b. Write **romantically**
        after b. Do NOT write **His look is** in c.

9. a. She smiles.
   b. She takes his arm.
   c. She walks away with him.

NOTE: Write ..., ..., **and** ....

10. a. They walk down the street together.
    b. People notice them.
    c. They look so happy.

NOTE: Use **As** before a. Write **because** before c.

11. a. Mr. and Mrs. Harras are going to dinner.
    b. They want to celebrate.
    c. The celebration is for their fifth wedding anniversary.

NOTE: Do NOT write **They want** in b. Do NOT write **The celebration is for** in c.

C. Reading Check

Circle the incorrect answer.

1. Mrs. Harras is (surprised,   attractive,   waiting for her husband,   standing on a corner).

2. The young man (invites her to dinner,   invites her for coffee,   looks at Mrs. Harras romantically,   walks away).

3. Mr. Harras (looks at his wife romantically,   invites his wife for a cup of coffee,   is taking his wife to dinner,   walks away with his wife).

4.   Mr. and Mrs. Harras (seem to have a happy marriage,   appear to love each other,   are both middle-aged,   are celebrating).

Who does each of the following words or phrases refer to? Place a check under the name of the person.

Words/Phrases	Young Man	Mrs. Harras	Mr. Harras
middle-aged			
handsome			
attractive			
says "hello"			
refuses politely			
invites for dinner			
invites for coffee			
on a corner			
surprised			
celebrating			
married			
walk away			

D.   Write Away

1.   Combine the sentences in Part B. Follow the suggestions in the *NOTES*. Write each group as one sentence. Do NOT write the numbers. After you finish, check your work with your teacher.

2.   Rewrite the paragraph in 1 above. Tell the story from Mrs. Harras' point of view. Change the story to *past tense*.

Your first sentence: **I was standing on the corner, and a handsome young man started to talk to me.**

E. Writing Follow-Up

Write a paragraph about wedding arrangements in your country. Give your paragraph a title. Answer these questions in your paragraph:

Who plans the marriage? (The woman? The man? The family?)

How old are the man and woman when they plan to marry?

Do the man and woman know each other well before the marriage? (How do they meet? Do they go out together before the marriage?)

What does the man pay for?

What does each family pay for?

What kinds of gifts do people give to the couple?

_____

_____

_____

_____

_____

_____

_____

_____

Unit 22

Working Together

A. Vocabulary Preview

Find the words in Part B that mean:

1. _refuse_ to say no; not to do, give, or accept

2. _____ an area that is different from sur-
rounding areas.

3. _____ very different; on a different side

4. _____ happening quickly

5. _____ a common low-growing green plant
eaten by many animals

B. Read the following:

Working Together

1. a. Zeke is a horse.
    b. Gus is a horse.

NOTE: Use **and**.

2. a. They work on a farm.
    b. The farm belongs to Mr. White.

NOTE: Use **, which** after a. Do NOT write **The farm**
in b.

3. a. Mr. White is angry with them.
    b. They refuse to work together.

NOTE: Use **because** after a.

4. a. One day he decides to teach them a lesson.
    b. The lesson is important.

5. a. He ties them together.
   b. He does this with a short rope.
   c. He ties it around their necks.

NOTE: Do NOT use **He does this** in b. nor **He ties it** in c.

6. a. He puts them between two patches of grass.
   b. The grass is fresh.
   c. The grass is green.

NOTE: Use **fresh, green** before **grass**. Do NOT write **The grass is** in b. and c.

7. a. Zeke looks at the grass on his side.
   b. He starts to walk to it.

8. a. Gus looks at the grass on his side.
   b. He starts to pull in that direction.

9. a. The short rope around their necks stops them.
   b. The stop is sudden.

NOTE: *Use* **suddenly** after a. Do NOT write b.

10. a. For a long time, they pull.
    b. They do this in opposite directions.

11. a. They get tired.
    b. They get hungry.

12. a. Then, they get an idea.
    b. They decide to try something different.

13. a. They walk together.
    b. They walk to one patch of grass.
    c. They eat it.

14. a. Then, they walk to the other patch of grass.
    b. They eat it.

15. a. Gus and Zeke now understand Mr. White's lesson:
    b. "Work together or starve."

C. Reading Check

After reading the sentences in Part B, decide whether these statements are *True (T)* or *False (F)*.

T   F   1. This story is about how working together can be helpful.

T   F   2. Mr. White, the farmer, does not know how to teach the two horses to work together.

T   F   3. The short rope makes it difficult for the two horses to pull in opposite directions.

T   F   4. The horses in this story are intelligent.

D. Write Away

1. Combine the sentences in Part B. Write each group as one sentence. Do NOT write the numbers. After you finish, check your work with your teacher.

2. Rewrite the story in the *past tense*.

Your first sentence: **Zeke and Gus were horses.**

E.   Writing Follow-Up

Write an animal story that teaches a lesson about life.

What is the animal?
What is the animal like?
What happens to the animal?
How does the animal learn a lesson?
What is the lesson the animal learns?
Is this lesson important for people?

_____

_____

_____

_____

_____

_____

_____

_____

Unit 23

The Car and The Mule

A.   Vocabulary Preview

Find the words in Part B that mean:

1. _laugh_   to make sounds with the voice to show happiness or disrespect.

2. _____ funny things said or done to make people laugh

3. _____ clever, having good sense

4. _____ to move the head up and down

5. _____ very small, powdery pieces of earth; dirt

6. _____ a long, narrow opening in the ground— for water beside a road

7. _____ to say how much someone will pay or give for something

B.   Read the following:

The Car and The Mule

1. a. Two young men are driving.
   b. They are driving in the country.

2. a. They pass a farmer.
   b. He is on a mule.

3. a. The young men point at the farmer.
   b. They are in the car.

NOTE: Add **in the car** after **men** in a. Omit **They are** in b.

4. a.   They laugh at him.
    b.   They make jokes.

5. a.   The farmer smiles.
    b.   His smile is wise.
    c.   He nods his head.

6. a.   The young men leave him behind.
    b.   He is in a cloud of dust.

7. a.   After a while, the farmer sees the men.
    b.   They are in the middle of the road.

8. a.   He also sees their car.
    b.   Their car is in a ditch.

9. a.   The men ask the farmer for help.
    b.   They want him to pull their car out of the
         ditch.

NOTE: Do NOT write **They want him** in b.

10. a.   The farmer laughs.
    b.   His laugh is loud.
    c.   The men are very ashamed.

11. a.   The men offer the farmer a lot of money.
    b.   They want him to pull their car out of the
         ditch.

NOTE: See 9 above.

12. a.   The farmer takes their money.
    b.   He pulls their car out with his mule.

13. He says, "Four legs are often better than four
    wheels."

C.   Reading Check

After reading the sentences in Part B, decide whether these statements are *True (T)* or *False (F)*. Circle the correct letter.

T   F   1. The young men in the car respect the farmer.

T   F   2. They laugh at the farmer because he is riding a mule.

T   F   3. The farmer is angry because the young men laugh at him.

T   F   4. The young men are driving on a modern highway.

T   F   5. The young men drive into a ditch along the road.

T   F   6. They offer money to the farmer for his help.

T   F   7. The farmer does not take their money.

D. Write Away

1. Combine the sentences in Part B. Write each group as one sentence. Do NOT write the numbers. After you finish, check your work with your teacher.

2. Rewrite the story in the *past tense.*

Your first sentence: **Two young men were driving in the country.**

E. Writing Follow-Up

What are some differences between country people and city people? Sometimes city people laugh at country people; sometimes country people laugh at city people. Do you know a funny story about city or country people? Write this story. Write your own title.

_____

_____

_____

_____

_____

_____

_____

Unit 24

Chickens for Sale

A.   Vocabulary Preview

Find the words in Part B that mean:

1. _*farm*_ a place for growing plants or raising animals

2. _____ a large food store where people serve themselves

3. _____ recently prepared or produced; not old

4. _____ the most delicious

5. _____ grow or produce

6. _____ tell people about something for sale in newspapers or on radio and television

7. _____ strong, not weak

8. _____ easy to eat or chew (like meat)

B.   Read the following:

Chickens for Sale

(1) I am a chicken farmer.   (2) I have a big chicken farm in the country.   (3) Each week I send thousands of chickens to supermarkets in large cities.   (4) My chickens are all fresh and unfrozen.   (5) I want to sell the freshest and tastiest chickens in the whole world. (6) I am a hardworking chicken farmer.   (7) I raise good chickens for people to eat.   (8) I advertise my chickens on television.   (9) I say, "It takes a tough man to make a tender chicken."

C.   Reading Check

After reading the paragraph in Part B, decide whether these statements are *True (T)* or *False (F)*. Circle the correct letter.

T   F   1. I have a large chicken farm and I sell eggs.

T   F   2. Many supermarkets in big cities sell my chickens.

T   F   3. My chickens are frozen.

T   F   4. I want to sell fresh, tasty, and tender chickens.

T   F   5. My life as a chicken farmer is easy.

T   F   6. I am on television.

D.   Write Away

1.   Rewrite the paragraph in Part B, changing the subject from **I** to **Frank Perdue**.

Your first sentence: **Frank Perdue is a chicken farmer.**

2.   Rewrite the paragraph in Part B, changing **I** to **Frank Perdue and his partner**.

Your first sentence: **Frank Perdue and his partner are chicken farmers**.

NOTE: In (9), change **a tough man** to **tough men** and **a tender chicken** to **tender chickens**.

3.   Rewrite the paragraph in Part B, changing the time to five years ago.

Your first sentence: **Five years ago Frank Perdue was a chicken farmer**.

NOTE: Do NOT change the words in quotation marks ("...") in (9).

4.   Go back to Exercise 1, **Frank Perdue is a chicken farmer**. Make a *yes* or *no* question for each sentence and give short answers.

Your first question and answer: **Is Frank Perdue a chicken farmer? Yes, he is**.

NOTE: Do NOT change the words in quotation marks ("...") in (9).

E.   Writing Follow-Up

Write a paragraph to describe your favorite advertisement on radio or television.

What product or service is the advertisement for?
When is the advertisement on the radio or TV?
How long is the advertisement?
Who appears in the advertisement?
Is the advertisement serious or funny? Why?
Why is it your favorite advertisement?

My Favorite Advertisement

_____

_____

_____

_____

_____

_____

_____

Unit 25

My Athens

A.   Vocabulary Preview

Find the word that is closest in meaning to the italicized word to the left. Draw a circle around it.

1. *live* (v.)   locate   (reside)   visit

2. *enjoy* (v.)   entertain   laugh   like

3. *view* (n.)   scene   sky   attraction

4. *frequently* (adv.)   often   rarely   seldom

5. *wonderful* (adj.)   beautiful   cheerful   terrific

6. *exciting* (adj.)   pleasing   thrilling   inviting

B.   Read the following:

My Athens

(1) I live in Athens, Greece.   (2) I enjoy this city and the friendly people here.   (3) I rent an apartment with three large windows near the Acropolis.   (4) From these windows, I have a view of the Acropolis and the Agora. (5) I frequently visit these places.   (6) Here I see many tourists from all over the world.   (7) I sometimes talk to these visitors.   (8) I tell them about the wonderful things in Athens.   (9) This is an exciting place!   (10) This is a beautiful city! (11) The Greeks are nice people!

C. Reading Check

After reading the paragraph in Part B, decide whether these statments are *True (T)*, *False (F)*, or *Unknown (U)*. Circle the correct letter.

T   F   U   1. I am a tourist in Greece.

T   F   U   2. For me, living in Athens is a pleasure.

T   F   U   3. I don't like all the tourists in Athens.

T   F   U   4. I speak Greek.

T   F   U   5. Quite often I visit some of the famous places in Athens.

T   F   U   6. My apartment is in a historical area.

D. Write Away

1. Rita also lives in Athens, Greece. Write about her.

Your first sentence: **Rita also lives in Athens, Greece.**

2. Last year I lived in Athens, Greece. Rewrite the paragraph in Part B in the *past tense*. Make all the necessary changes (here, this, these).

Your first sentence: **Last year I lived in Athens, Greece.**

3.   Rewrite the paragraph in Part B by inserting the following words in the sentences. Omit the numbers.

In (1), **sunny** before **Athens**
In (2), **truly** before **enjoy**
In (3), **lovely** before **apartment**
In (4), **fantastic** before **view**
In (5), **historic** before **places**
In (6), **often** before **see**
In (7), **excited** before **visitors**
In (8), **many** before **wonderful**
In (9), **very** before **exciting**
In (10), **extremely** before **beautiful**
In (11), **unusually** before **nice**

E. Writing Follow-Up

Write an article for a travel magazine about your favorite
city.

What is the name of the city?
Where is it?
What is it like?
What are some famous places to visit?
What is the climate like?
What are the people like?
Why do you like this city?

My Favorite City

_____

_____

_____

_____

_____

_____

_____

Unit 26

The Fortuneteller

A.   Vocabulary Preview

Find the words in Part B that mean:

1. *fortuneteller* someone who says he/she can look into the future.

2. _____ someone who buys goods or services from a shop or a person

3. _____ statements about the future

4. _____ the inside surface of the hand

5. _____ to mix up something, usually cards, to allow for a chance order

6. _____ a round, glass object

B.   Read the following:

The Fortuneteller

(1) Madame Fifi isn't a rich fortuneteller.   (2) She doesn't have many customers.   (3) She isn't very serious about her work.   (4) Her predictions aren't always true.   (5) She can't read palms very well.   (6) She doesn't read tea leaves.   (7) She doesn't know how to shuffle cards.   (8) She can't see the future in her crystal ball.   (9) She isn't able to make a good living as a fortuneteller.   (10) She has to find a new job.   (11) She'll become a belly dancer.

C.   Reading Check

After reading the sentences in Part B, decide whether these statements are *True (T)* or *False (F)*. Circle the correct letter.

T   F   1. Madame Fifi isn't a successful fortuneteller.

T   F   2. She is very dedicated and capable.

T   F   3. Seeing the future in her crystal ball is easy for her.

T   F   4. She knows what her new job will be.

T   F   5. She handles cards skillfully.

T   F   6. She has *four* ways to tell the future.

D.   Write Away

1.   Fill in the blanks in these questions and answers about Madame Fifi. Use the information in Part B, as shown in the example for sentence (1).

(1) **Isn't** Madame Fifi a rich fortuneteller? No, she **isn't**.

(2) _____ she _____ many customers?

No, she _____.

(3) _____ she very serious about her work? No,

she _____.

(4) _____ her predictions always true? No, they _____.

(5) _____ she _____ palms very well? No, she _____.

(6) _____ she _____ tea leaves? No, she _____.

(7) _____ she know how to shuffle cards? No, she _____.

(8) _____ she _____ the future in her crystal ball? No, she _____.

(9) _____ she able to make a good living as a fortuneteller? No, she _____.

(10) _____ she _____ to find a new job? Yes, she _____

(11) _____ she _____ a belly dancer? Yes, she _____.

2. Madame Zara is a successful fortuneteller. Write about her using the information in Part B as a model.

Your first sentence: **Madame Zara is a rich fortuneteller.**

NOTE: Omit (11).

3.   Look at the questions about Madame Fifi in D.1,
above, and write similar questions and answers about
Madame Zara.

Your first question and answer: **Is Madame Zara a
rich fortuneteller? Yes, she is.**

4.   Roy Raindrop is a weatherman on TV, but he is not a
very good one. Rewrite the paragraph in Part B and
make the following changes. Do NOT change (3) and
(10).

In (1), change **rich fortuneteller** to **good weatherman**
In (2), change **customers** to **viewers**
In (4), insert **weather** before **predictions**
In (5), change **palms** to **a thermometer**
In (6), change **tea leaves** to **weather charts**
In (7), change **shuffle cards** to **draw maps**
In (8), change **see ... ball** to **forecast the next
    day's weather**
In (9), change **fortuneteller** to **weatherman**
In (11), change **belly dancer** to **linguists**

Your first sentence: **Roy Raindrop isn't a very
good weatherman.**

5.   Rewrite the paragraph in Part B making the following changes. Omit the numbers.

Combine (1) and (2) with **because.**
Combine (3) and (4) with **, and.**
Combine (5) and (6) with **, and.** Write **at all** after (6).
Combine (7) and (8) with **, and.** Write **very well** after (7).
    Insert **even** after **can't** in (8).
Combine (9) and (10) with **so** after (9). Before (9),
    write **Obviously,...**
Do NOT change (11).

E.   Writing Follow-Up

Many people believe that it is possible to look into the
future. Write a story about a prediction that came true.
Include answers to the questions that follow.

What was the prediction?
Who made the prediction?
How did that person predict the future? (Cards? Tea
*   leaves? Crystal ball? Palm reading?)*
What happened?
How did the prediction come true?
How long did it take before the prediction came true?
How did people feel about the prediction?

_____

_____

_____

_____

_____

_____

_____

_____

Unit 27

The Holdup

A.   Vocabulary Preview

These words are in Part B. Match each word with its definition. (There is one definition that does not match any word.)

_d_   1. handle (v.)

_____   2. shake

_____   3. growl

_____   4. congratulate

_____   5. pat

_____   6. teller

_____   7. blind

a. an animal's low sound in the throat to show anger

b. touch gently with the hand to show praise

c. complain; to show anger or unhappiness

d. feel with the hands; move by hand

e. move quickly up and down, forwards and backwards

f. express praise or admiration for something done successfully

g. unable to see

h. a job in a bank

B.   Read the following:

The Holdup

1. a. Alice works in a bank.
   b. The bank is in the city.

2. a. She is a teller.
   b. She handles a lot of money.

NOTE: Use **who** after a. Do NOT write **She** in b.

3. a. She likes her job.
    b. She is afraid of bank robbers.

NOTE: Use **, but** after a.

4. a. One day a woman comes to her window.
    b. The woman is well-dressed.
    c. The woman gives her a note.

5. a. Alice reads the note.
    b. She begins to shake with fear.

6. a. The woman is a bank robber.
    b. She wants all of Alice's money.

7. a. Alice puts the money in a bag.
    b. She gives it to the woman.

8. a. The woman turns.
    b. The turn is quick.
    c. She walks toward the door.

9. a. At that moment a blind man enters the bank.
    b. At that moment his Seeing Eye dog enters the bank.

10. a. The dog sees the woman.
     b. He starts to growl.
     c. He starts to show his teeth.

11. a. The woman drops the bag of money.
     b. She is afraid of the dog.

NOTE: Use **because** after a.

12. a. She tries to run away.
     b. The dog stops her.

NOTE: Use **, but** after a.

13. a. Alice calls the bank guard.
     b. He takes the woman to the police station.

NOTE: Use **, who** after a. Do NOT write **He** in b.

14. a. The people congratulate the blind man.
     b. They are in the bank.
     c. They pat his dog on the head.

15. a. He tells them his dog used to be a police dog.
     b. The police gave him away.
     c. He was too friendly.

NOTE: Use **, but** after a. Use **because** after b.

C.   Reading Check

Give each sentence a number, beginning with 1, 2, 3, etc.,
to show the order in the story.

_____   a. Alice calls the bank guard, who comes and
            takes the bank robber to the police station.

___1___ b. At the same time, a blind man with a Seeing
            Eye dog enters the bank, and the dog growls
            at the robber.

_____   c. One day a well-dressed woman gives her a
            note that asks for all her money.

_____ d. Alice likes her job as a bank teller, but she is afraid of bank robbers.

_____ e. The bank robber walks towards the door.

_____ f. Alice puts the money in a bag and gives it to the woman.

_____ g. The man tells the people that his dog was too friendly to be a police dog.

_____ h. The woman drops the bag of money and tries to run away, but the dog stops her.

D.   Write Away

1.   Combine the sentences in Part B. Write each group as one sentence. Do NOT write the numbers. After you finish, check your work with your teacher.

2.   Rewrite the paragraph in Exercise 1 above. Tell the story of *The Holdup* in the past tense.

Your first sentence: **Alice worked in a bank in the city**.

E.   Writing Follow-Up

Select one of the following topics and write a paragraph with your own title.

1.   You work for a newspaper. Write the story in Part B as a news article. Give all information to answer *who, what, when, where, how, why.*

2.   Write a newspaper article about another crime, an accident, or a fire that you saw. Answer *who, what, when, where, how,* and *why.*

_____

_____

_____

_____

_____

_____

_____

_____

Unit 28

An Outdoor Market

A.   Vocabulary Preview

Find the words in Part B that mean:

1. *atmosphere* a feeling you get from a place

2. _____ not in order; mixed up

3. _____ a number of different things

4. _____ cooked in an oven

5. _____ a large food shop where people serve themselves

B.   Read the following:

An Outdoor Market

(1) An outdoor market is an interesting place in the summer. (2) There is a busy atmosphere. (3) Also, there is a lot of noise. (4) There is a lot of confusion. (5) There is a lot of color in the various areas. (6) There are fresh carrots, tomatoes, and cucumbers in the vegetable area. (7) In the fruit area, there are apples and oranges. (8) There are breads, cookies, and pies in the bakery area. (9) In the dairy area, there are fresh eggs, milk, and cheese. (10) There are sausages, meat, and fish in the butcher area. (11) In the poultry area, there are chickens, ducks, and geese. (12) There is a big difference between an outdoor market and a supermarket.

C. Reading Check

The items in Column A belong in the different areas in an outdoor market listed in Column B. Write the items from Column A under the correct area in Column B.

Column A	Column B	
cucumbers	*vegetable area*	*fruit area*
ducks		
cheese		
fish		
bread	*bakery area*	*dairy area*
oranges		
carrots		
cakes		
sausages	*butcher area*	*poultry area*
apples		
chickens		
milk		

D.   Write Away

1.   Rewrite the paragraph, using contractions for **is**. Do NOT use contractions for **are**.

Your first sentence: **An outdoor market's an interesting place in the summer.**

2.   Ask questions about an outdoor market, following the sentence order in Part B.

Your first question: **Is an outdoor market an interesting place in the summer?**

NOTE: In sentences (6) through (11) add **any**.

3.   It is winter and the market is closed. Write about it.

Your first sentence: **An outdoor market isn't an interesting place in the winter.**

NOTE: In sentences (6) through (11) add **any**. Omit (12).

4.   There are other areas of an outdoor market, some of which are listed below. Write five sentences with **There are** and five sentences with **There is**.

EXAMPLES: **There is a shoe repair shop in an out-door market. There are dishes in an outdoor market.**

shoes	water fountain
tailor	fabric shop
glasses	sheets
flowers	towels
flower shop	spice shop
notary public	buttons
socks	needlework store

5.   Rewrite the paragraph in Part B. Omit the numbers.

Combine (1) and (2) with **because of the**. Do NOT write
      There is a in (2).
Combine (3), (4), and (5) with . . . , . . . , **and** . . . . Do NOT
      write **There is a lot of** in (4) and (5).
Combine (6) and (7) with **, and**.
Combine (8) and (9) with **, and**.
Combine (10) and (11) with **, while**.
Do NOT change (12).

E.   Writing Follow-Up

Write a paragraph that describes the area around your house, apartment, or school. Use *there is* and *there are* and such words as *next to, between, to the left (right) of, across from, on the corner.* Mention: *post office, library, shops and stores (what kinds?), hospital, service stations, restaurants, parks, churches or other houses of worship.*

You can use one of the following sentences to begin your paragraph.

1. **My school is on a busy street. There are (is) . . . .**

2. **My apartment (home) is on a quiet (busy) street. There are (is) . . . .**

_____

_____

_____

_____

_____

_____

_____

_____

Unit 29

The Matter of ?

A. Vocabulary Preview

Find the words in Part B that mean:

1. _extra_ more than what is usual or expected

2. _____ a sign, a mark, or an object that repre-
    sents something

3. _____ a shorter form of a word, often used
    in writing

4. _____ not suddenly; little by little; slowly

5. _____ joining or putting together

B.   Read the following:

The Matter of ?

1. a.   The question mark has a history.
    b.   Its history is interesting.

2. a.   It comes from Roman times.
    b.   In Roman times people spoke Latin.

NOTE: Use , **when** after a. Do NOT write **In Roman
    times** in b.

3. a.   In Latin you had to add a word.
    b.   The word was extra.
    c.   You did this to ask a question.

4. a.   You had to add *Quaestio.*
    b.   You added it at the end of the sentence.

5. a. People wrote questions.
    b. They wrote a symbol.
    c. The symbol looked like the number "2" beside an "o" [*2o*].

NOTE: Use **When** before a. Use **that** after b. Do NOT write **The symbol** in c.

6. a. This symbol represented *Qo.*
    b. The *Qo* was an abbreviation for *Quaestio.*

NOTE: Use **, which** after a. Do NOT write **The Qo** in b.

7. a. Later people put the "2" over the "o" [*²ᵒ*].
    b. The "o" gradually became a dot [.].

NOTE: See 6 above.

8. a. This combination became the question mark [?].
    b. We write it today.

NOTE: See 6 above.

C. Reading Check

After reading the sentences in Part B, decide whether these statements are *True (T)* or *False (F)*. Circle the correct letter.

T   F   1. To ask a question in Roman times, you had to add an extra word at the beginning of the sentence.

T   F   2. The added word came from Latin.

T   F   3. In Latin, the word *Quaestio* was written to show a question.

T   F   4. Writers in Roman times abbreviated *Quaestio* to Qu.

T   F   5. Slowly Qo became a "2" over an "o" and finally today's question mark.

T   F   6. 2 and Q look alike in written English.

D. Write Away

Combine the sentences in Part B. Write each group as one sentence. Do NOT write the numbers. After you finish, check your work with your teacher.

E.   Writing Follow-Up

Choose one of the following and write about it. Give a title to your composition.

1. Some words have interesting histories. Select three of the following words: *assassin, chauvinism, shampoo, tantalize, diesel (engine), sabotage.*

    Look them up in a good English-language dictionary, then write about their origins and how they are used today. Go to a library if necessary. Use the following reference books to find information about the origin of the words you have chosen:

    A Short Etymological Dictionary of Modern English
        by Eric Partridge (Macmillan Company, 1958)
    Webster's Third New International Dictionary
        (Unabridged)
    The American Heritage Dictionary of the English
        Language (Houghton Mifflin Company)
    Complete Oxford English Dictionary

2. Write a paragraph to describe your country's flag. Give as much information as you can.

    What is the design of your flag?
    How did that design develop?
    How has the design changed through history?
    Do the design and colors have any special meanings?
        (For example, the 50 stars in the U.S. flag repre-
        sent the 50 states.)
    How do people feel about your flag?

_____

_____

_____

_____

_____

_____

_____

_____

_____

Unit 30

The Judo
Teacher

A.   Vocabulary Preview

1. Find the words in Part B that are the *opposite* of
   the following:

   a. late   *early*

   b. dull, boring   _____

   c. careless   _____

   d. stale, old   _____

   e. beginning   _____

   f. empty   _____

2. Write the *past tense* form of these irregular verbs:

Present Form	Past Form
a. teach	*taught*
b. catch	
c. think	
d. seek	
e. bring	
f. buy	
g. fight	

B.   Read the following:

The Judo Teacher

(1) Barbara teaches judo in secondary school.   (2) She catches the early bus to school every day.   (3) On the bus she thinks about her students.   (4) She seeks ways to make her classes more interesting.   (5) She brings her lunch every day.   (6) With her lunch she has a glass of milk.   (7) She buys it in the cafeteria.   (8) She is careful about her health.   (9) She only eats fresh food. (10) At the end of the day, she fights to get on the crowded bus.   (11) She uses her judo skill to get a seat.

C. Reading Check

After reading the paragraph in Part B, decide whether these statements are *True (T)* or *False (F)*. Circle the correct letter. Which sentence from the story helped you decide? Write the number of the sentence in the space provided.

(T)   F   __4__   1. Barbara is a serious teacher.

T   F   _____   2. She does not think about how to make students like her class.

T   F   _____   3. She drives her car to school every day.

T   F   _____   4. She buys her lunch in the cafeteria.

T   F   _____   5. There are lots of people on the bus in the evening, but Barbara never has to stand up.

T   F   _____   6. Barbara's students are adults.

D.   Write Away

1.   Ben is a boxing teacher in Barbara's school. Write about him.

Your first sentence: **Ben teaches boxing in a secondary school.**

NOTE: In (11), change **judo** to **boxing**.

2.   Barbara changed her job last year and no longer teaches judo. Rewrite the paragraph in the *past tense.*

Your first sentence: **Barbara taught judo in a secondary school.**

3.   Write questions about Barbara's past. Use the paragraph from Exercise 2.

Your first sentence: **Did Barbara teach judo in a secondary school?**

4.   Rewrite the paragraph in Part B, making the following changes. Omit the numbers.

Combine (1) and (2) with **, and.**
Combine (3) and (4) with **, and.**
Do NOT change (5).
Combine (6) and (7) with **, which.**

NOTE: In (7), omit **it.**

Before (8), put **Because** and combine it with (9).
Combine (10) and (11) with **, and.**

E. Writing Follow-Up

Write a letter to a friend and tell him/her about your job. (If you do not work, write about someone else's job.) Include the answers to the following questions:

What do you do?
When/how do you go to work?
Where do you eat lunch?
What do you have for lunch?
Why do you have that for lunch?
What do you like/dislike about your job?
When do you go home?
How do you travel?

_____

_____,

_____

_____

_____

_____

_____

_____

_____

_____

_____

_____

Unit 31
The House Husband

A.   Vocabulary Preview

These words are in Part B. Match each word with its definition. (There is one definition that does not match any word.)

_*d*_   1. vacuum (v.)

_____   2. knock (v.)

_____   3. answer (v.)

_____   4. realize (v.)

_____   5. prepare (v.)

_____   6. irritated (adj.)

a. understand and believe (a fact)

b. angry or annoyed

c. get something ready for use or for a purpose

d. clean by using a machine that pulls the dirt into a bag

e. give something for money

f. say something in response to a question

g. hit something to make a noise to get someone's attention

B.   Read the following:

The House Husband

1. a.   Eric washed the dishes.
    b.   Eric made the beds.
    c.   Eric vacuumed the rugs.

2. a.   Later he talked with a friend.
    b.   He talked on the telephone.

3. a.   In the afternoon, someone knocked.
    b.   The knock was on the door.

4. a.   It was a salesman.
    b.   He was selling vacuum cleaners.

5. a.   The salesman asked for the lady of the house.
    b.   Eric answered, "She isn't here."

6. a.   The salesman left.
    b.   Eric looked at his watch.
    c.   He realized he was late.

NOTE: Use **After** before a.

7. a.   Dinner had to be ready at six.
    b.   He had to prepare it.

8. a.   Dinner was ready.
    b.   He set the table.
    c.   He waited for Lucia.
    d.   She is his wife.

NOTE: Use **When** before a.

9.   a.   At exactly five, Lucia came in.
      b.   Eric gave her a cup of coffee.

10.   a.   She was tired.
      b.   She was irritated.
      c.   It was after her long day as a traffic
          policewoman.
      d.   She was happy to be home.

NOTE: Use **, but** after c.

C. Reading Check

Give each sentence a number, beginning with 1, 2, 3, etc.,
to show the order in the story.

_____   a. A salesman knocked on the door and wanted
          to talk to the lady of the house.

_____   b. At 5 o'clock his tired wife, Lucia, arrived home
          after a busy day as a traffic policewoman.

_____   c. Then, he talked to a friend on the
          telephone.

_____   d. He realized it was time to prepare dinner for
          six o'clock.

_____   e. Eric said the lady of the house wasn't
          there.

_____   f. He set the table and waited for his wife to
          arrive home.

_____   g. Eric washed the dishes, made the beds, and
          cleaned the house.

D.   Write Away

1.   Combine the sentences in Part B. Write each group as one sentence. Do NOT write the numbers. After you finish, check your work with your teacher.

2.   Rewrite the story from Eric's point of view.

Your first sentence: **I washed the dishes,** . . . .

E.   Writing Follow-Up

Select one of the following topics and write a paragraph. Give your paragraph a title.

1.   Do you know a man or a woman who has an unusual job? Describe the kind of work that he or she does or did.

2.   Describe a famous woman in your country's history. What did she do to become famous.

3.   Describe what a housewife (or house husband) has to do to take care of a house and family. Mention cleaning, cooking, shopping, and other duties.

_____

_____

_____

_____

_____

_____

_____

_____

Unit 32

Let's Eat

A. Vocabulary Preview

Find the words in Part B that mean:

1. ___*share*___ have, use, or take part in with another person or others

2. _____ a chance or duty to do something alternating with another person or people.

3. _____ give food to people

4. _____ cooked food of some kind served on a plate

5. _____ the meat of farm cattle, cut into very tiny pieces (two words)

6. _____ a set of names or things written one after the other

7. _____ do something quickly

8. _____ food or seasonings in a recipe

9. _____ speak in an unhappy, dissatisfied way

B.   Read the following:

(1) Pablo shares an apartment with two friends.   (2) Tonight, it's his turn to fix dinner.   (3) He wants to serve *chili con carne* with rice.   (4) It's quick and easy to prepare.   (5) He finds some rice in a box.   (6) There isn't enough for three people.   (7) There aren't any beans. (8) There aren't any onions, either.   (9) In the refrigerator, he finds some chopped beef and some celery. (10) There aren't any tomatoes.   (11) He almost forgets the chili powder.   (12) He finds some on a shelf above the stove.   (13) He makes a list of the ingredients he needs.   (14) He hurries to the supermarket to buy them. (15) His friends are always hungry when they come home.   (16) They complain a lot if dinner isn't ready.

C. Reading Check

After reading the paragraph in Part B, decide whether these statements are *True (T), False (B),* or *Unknown (U).* Circle the correct letter.

T F U   1. There are three people in Pablo's house.

T F U   2. He always cooks dinner for his two friends.

T F U   3. He only knows how to prepare *chili con carne.*

T F U   4. He finds everything he needs to make *chili con carne.*

T F U   5. Before he goes shopping, he makes a list of things he needs to buy.

T F U   6. His friends love *chili con carne.*

T F U   7. They are unhappy when dinner is late.

T F U   8. Pablo and his friends always eat together.

D.   Write Away

1.   Pablo is married now and lives with his wife. Write about him in the *past tense*.

Your first sentence: **Last year, Pablo shared an apartment with two friends.**

NOTE: In (2), change **Tonight** to **One night**.

2.   Lola wants to bake a chocolate cake, but she doesn't have all the ingredients that she needs. She makes one list (List A) of the ingredients she has and another list (List B) of the ingredients she doesn't have.

List A	List B
salt	sugar
flour	cocoa
butter	vanilla
milk	eggs
baking soda	

Use the words from List A and write three sentences of your own with **some**; then use the words from List B and write three sentences with **any**. Remember to use a negative word (**not**) with **any**. Two examples follow:

List A

Lola has **some** salt.

_____

_____

_____

_____

List B

She does**n't** have **any** sugar.

_____

_____

_____

_____

3. Rewrite the paragraph in Part B by combining the following sentences. Omit the numbers.

(1) and (2) with **, and**
(3) and (4) with **because**
(5) and (6) with **, but**
(7) and (8) with **, and**
(9) and (10) with **, but**
(11) and (12) with **, but**
(13) and (14) with **, and**
(15) and (16) with **, and**

E.   Writing Follow-Up

Write a paragraph about one of the following topics.
Give your paragraph a title.

1.   Have you ever shared an apartment or a house with a
     friend or friends? Was it a good or a bad experience?
     Give some examples to show why it was good or bad.
     Don't forget to describe your friend or friends.

2.   Do you know how to prepare a simple dish that your
     family and friends like? Describe how you make it.

3.   *Wanted: A Roommate.* Pretend that you are looking
     for a roommate to share your apartment or house.
     You want to put a notice on the bulletin board at
     school or at work. Describe the apartment (or house)
     and describe the type of person you are looking for
     including any shared housekeeping duties. Include
     the amount of money you will charge for rent.

Unit 33
Moving In

A.   Vocabulary Preview

Find the words in Part B that mean:

1. _recently_ not long ago

2. _____ a group of people and their homes in a small area within a town or city

3. _____ people who live near each other

4. _____ located beside another house (two words)

5. _____ a shop where medicine is sold, also known as a drugstore

6. _____ a person who fits and repairs water pipes

7. _____ goods for the home and garden

B.   Read the following:

Moving In

Martha and Richard recently moved into a new neighborhood. They needed to learn a lot of things. Therefore, they made a list of questions to ask their next-door neighbors.

1. *Where is the nearest supermarket?*
2. *What is the name of the best elementary school in the neighborhood?*
3. *What is the address of the closest pharmacy?*
4. *Who is the most reliable plumber in the area?*
5. *How far is the nearest bus stop?*
6. *What is the name and address of the best doctor nearby?*
7. *Where is the nearest hardware store?*
8. *What is the name of the most popular restaurant?*

C. Reading Check

After reading the paragraph in Part B, decide whether these statements are *True (T)*, *False (F)*, or *Probably True (PT)*. Circle the correct answer.

T   F   PT   1. Martha and Richard are married.

T   F   PT   2. They want information about their next-door neighbors.

T   F   PT   3. Before they moved, Martha and Richard were familiar with their new neighborhood.

T   F   PT   4. Martha and Richard have one child or more children.

T   F   PT   5. They do not have a car

T   F   PT   6. Their neighbors gave them the information.

D. Write Away

1.   Write the questions listed in Part B, but begin each one with **Can you please tell me . . . ?**

Your first sentence: **Can you please tell me where the nearest supermarket is?**

NOTE: Notice that the question word order changes when it becomes a noun clause.

2.   Write the same questions, but begin each one with
Do you know ... ?

Your first question: **Do you know where the nearest
supermarket is?**

3.   Hector, one of the next-door neighbors, had just recently moved into the neighborhood, too, so he could not
give any information to Martha and Richard. Write his
answers. Begin each one with **I don't know ....**

Your first sentence: **I don't know where the nearest
supermarket is.**

4.   Danny is 21 years old. He has a new job in a bank, but
he is not a very serious employee. These are some questions that he plans to ask on his first day of work.

   a. *Where's my private office?*
   b. *Who's my secretary.*
   c. *Where's the executive dining room?*
   d. *What's the name of the brunette vice-president.*
   e. *When's the next bank holiday?*
   f. *When's the next office party?*

Rewrite Danny's questions but begin each one with
Could you tell me ... ?

Your first question: **Could you tell me where my
private office is?**

5.   The security guard at the bank could not answer any
of Danny's questions. Write his answers. Begin each one
with **I'm not sure ....**

Your first answer: **I'm not sure where your private
office is.**

E.   Writing Follow-Up

Write about your experiences when you moved to a new
neighborhood, city, or country. Give your paragraph a
title. Include the answers to the following questions:

Where did you move to?
What kinds of information did you need?
What kind of neighborhood was it?
What was in that neighborhood? (Look back at Part B.)
How did the neighbors treat you?

_____

_____

_____

_____

_____

_____

_____

Unit 34

Dead Men Tell No Tales

A.   Vocabulary Preview

These words are in Part B. Match each word with its definition. (There is one definition that does not match any word.)

_g_ 1. grave

_____ 2. coastal

_____ 3. dig

_____ 4. foundation

_____ 5. skeleton

_____ 6. supervisor

_____ 7. notify

_____ 8. archeologist

_____ 9. examine

a. the basis on which something is built

b. not pleasant because of death and destruction

c. look closely to find out something

d. a person who watches over work and workers and tells them what to do

e. next to the sea

f. scientist who studies objects from ancient times

g. the place in the ground where dead people are buried

h. break up, turn over, or remove earth

i. tell someone in a formal way

j. the bone framework of a human or animal body

B.   Read the following:

Dead Men Tell No Tales

1. a. In 1969 a mass grave was found.
    b. It was found in a coastal city.
    c. The coastal city was south of Rome.

2. a. Some construction workers were digging.
    b. They were digging a foundation.
    c. The foundation was for a factory.

3. a. They found skeletons.
    b. There were 50.
    c. They were of young men.
    d. The young men were 6 feet, 7 inches tall.

NOTE: Use **,** **who** after c. Do NOT write **The young men**
          in d.

4. a. The supervisor notified the officials.
    b. He supervised the workers.
    c. The officials were in the government.

NOTE: Use **of** after **supervisor** in a.

5. a. Immediately, the archeologists arrived.
    b. They were from Rome.
    c. They arrived to examine the mass grave.
    d. They arrived to examine the skeletons.

6. a. They said the men died during the Roman
        Empire.
    b. They were in good health.
    c. The good health was at the time of their death.

7. a. They had strong bones.
    b. They had strong teeth.

8. a. The archeologists could not answer some
        questions.
    b. The questions were important.

9. a. Who were these men?
    b. What caused their deaths?
    c. Their deaths happened at the same time.
    d. Their deaths happened in the same place.

C. Reading Check

Give each sentence a number, beginning with 1, 2, 3, etc.,
to show the order in which these things happened.

_____ a. Archeologists from Rome came to examine
           the skeletons.

_____ b. They found the mass grave with the skeletons
           of the 50 men.

__1__   c. Some time during the Roman Empire,
           something caused the deaths of 50 men.

_____ d. They also said the men had been in good
           health at the time of death.

_____ e. After their deaths, they were all buried in
           a large grave.

_____ f. The archeologists could not, however,
           explain the cause of death or why they
           were buried together.

___ g. In 1969, workers were digging a foundation.

___ h. They said the men were young and tall.

D.   Write Away

Combine the sentences in Part B. Write each group as one sentence. Do not write the numbers. After you finish, check your work with your teacher.

E.   Writing Follow-Up

Do *both* of these writing assignments.

1. With a classmate, write an ending to "Dead Men Tell No Tales." Try to solve the mystery of who the 50 men were and what caused their death. Use your imagination and give as many details as you can. Share your ending with your classmates. Use the expressions below if necessary.

2. Do you know a mystery story? Write it. Be sure to explain carefully everything that happened. Do you think you know what really happened? Use the expressions below if necessary.

Possibly . . . .
Probably . . . .
Perhaps . . . .
Maybe . . . .

_____

_____

_____

_____

_____

_____

_____

_____

_____

Unit 35

An Endangered Species

A.   Vocabulary Preview

1.   These words are in Part B. Match each word with its definition.

_____C_____ 1. species

_____ 2. endangered

_____ 3. poacher

_____ 4. horn

_____ 5. handle (n.)

_____ 6. dagger

_____ 7. rhinoceros

_____ 8. 200

a. a hard, pointed growth, usually on the top of an animal's head, sometimes at the end of a long nose (snout)

b. a short, pointed knife used as a weapon

c. a group of plants or animals that are of the same kind

d. a part of an object specially made for holding it

e. a large horned animal that eats grass

f. a person who catches or kills animals without permission

g. caused danger to

h. a place for wild animals (in a big city)

2.   Match the words in Column A with their opposites in Column B.

	Column A	Column B
_C_	1. ancestor	a. feminine
_____	2. ancient	b. passive
_____	3. energetic	c. descendant
_____	4. masculine	d. stay
_____	5. roam	e. modern
_____	6. adult	f. immature

B.   Read the following:

An Endangered Species

1.   a.   The rhinoceros has ancestors.
    b.   They are ancient.
    c.   They lived all over the world.
    d.   They lived 60 million years ago.

NOTE: Use **that** after a.

2.   a.   Today, the rhinoceros is a species.
    b.   Today, the rhinoceros is endangered.

3.   a.   Only a few hundred of them are alive.
    b.   They are alive in game parks.
    c.   The game parks are in Africa and Asia.
    d.   Others are alive in zoos.

4.   a.   Rhinoceros* are disappearing.
    b.   Poachers are killing them
    c.   The killing is for their horns.
    d.   The horns are valuable.

NOTE: Use **because** after a.

5.   a.   In Asia, older men pay a lot of money.
    b.   The money is for a powder.
    c.   The powder is made from the horns.
    d.   The horns come from adult rhinoceros.

6.   a.   These men believe this powder gives them the power.
    b.   This power is to feel young.
    c.   This power is to feel strong.
    d.   This power is to feel energetic.

7.   a.   There are some wealthy men in some Middle Eastern countries.
    b.   They pay a lot of money.
    c.   The money is for the horns of rhinoceros.

*Most dictionaries list Rhinoceros as both singular and plural.

8. a. These men use the horns.
    b. They use them as handles.
    c. The handles are on daggers.
    d. The daggers are called *jambias*.

NOTE: Use **, which** after c.

9. a. To own a *jambia* is a sign.
    b. The sign is of power.
    c. The power is masculine.

10. a. In 1969, there were 18,000 rhinoceros.
    b. They roamed freely.
    c. They were in Kenya.
    d. Kenya is in Africa.
    e. In 1981, there were only 1000 left.

11. a. The rhinoceros is in danger.
    b. The danger is of disappearing forever.
    c. Some men can feel young.
    d. Other men can feel powerful.

NOTE: Use **just so that** after b. Use **or** after c.

C. Reading Check

After reading the sentences in Part B, decide whether these statements are *True (T)* or *False (F)*. Circle the correct letter.

T   F   1. Rhinoceros have lived on the earth for only a short time.

T   F   2. From 1969 to 1981 many rhinoceros were killed in Kenya.

T   F   3. Poachers kill rhinoceros because they are dangerous animals.

T   F   4. Men all over the world are willing to pay a lot of money for the horns of rhinoceros.

T   F   5. The horns of rhinoceros are used to make a medicine for very sick people.

T   F   6. Rhinoceros are an endangered species.

T   F   7. The poachers only want the horn of the rhinoceros.

T   F   8. The only wild rhinoceros left are in Africa.

D.   Write Away

Combine the sentences in Part B. Write each group as one sentence. Do not write the numbers. After you finish, check your work with your teacher.

E.   Writing Follow-Up

There are many other animals in danger of disappearing from earth. (Some other endangered species are elephants, which are killed for their ivory tusks, and seals, which are killed for their fur.) Write a letter to the editor of a newspaper. Use the form on the next page or use your own paper. Include answers to the following questions:

What is the animal?
Why is it an endangered species?
How many animals are there?
Where does it live?
Why do people kill it?
How can we save the animal?
What can each person do to keep these animals safe?

_____

_____ ,

_____

_____

_____

_____

_____

_____

_____

_____

_____

Grammatical Index